Successful SAP R/3 Implementation

Successful SAP R/3 Implementation

Practical management of ERP projects

Norbert Welti

Addison-Wesley

Harlow, England • Reading, Massachusetts • Menlo Park, California
New York • Don Mills, Ontario • Amsterdam • Bonn • Sydney • Singapore
Tokyo • Madrid • San Juan • Milan • Mexico City • Seoul • Taipei

Addison Wesley Longman Limited
Edinburgh Gate
Harlow
Essex CM20 2JE
England

and Associated Companies throughout the World.

Cover designed by Senate
Typeset in 9.5/12 StoneSerif by 43
Printed and bound in The United States of America.

First printed 1999

ISBN 0-201-39824-9

British Library Cataloguing-in-Publication Data
A catalogue record for this book is available from the British Library

It must be considered that there is nothing more difficult to carry out, nor more doubtful of success, nor more dangerous to handle, than to initiate a new order of things. For the reformer has enemies in all those who profit by the old order, and only lukewarm defenders in all those who would profit by the new order, this lukewarmness arising partly from fear of their adversaries, who have the laws in their favour; and partly from the incredulity of mankind, who do not truly believe in anything new until they have actual experience of it.

Niccolò Machiavelli
The Prince

Foreword

This book is on implementing Enterprise Resources Planning (ERP) packages with standardized software (SAP R/3) in a relatively complex (multi-site, multi-country) environment.

As a manager in industry and later as a consultant partner with PricewaterhouseCoopers, I specialized in supply-chain management, and have the experience of many projects to draw on for comparisons. The project that forms the focus for the case study in this book was very well managed by the company management, especially the CEO of ALVEO, Dr Jean-Pierre Sormani, and the overall project manager, Norbert Welti. The project was remarkable in three senses:

- It met its objectives.
- It finished on schedule – earlier, even.
- It stayed within budget.

Norbert Welti draws on this experience – and his further extensive experience with project management and business process reorganization, including 10 years within SAP implementation – and shares it with you in this book.

This book will help professionals in sales and marketing, manufacturing, supply-chain management, finance and accounting that come across an ERP implementation. It will be especially useful to project managers and leaders of ERP projects, ERP software teams and such like. It will help these professionals and project managers to:

- Avoid pitfalls in a project.
- Organize, manage, and lead a project effectively and efficiently.
- Implement an ERP project and its standard software on schedule and within budget.

For me it was a pleasure and an honor to be close to the birth of this practical and down-to-earth book. It is a great book and I hope that my colleagues in industry, in consulting and in universities will harvest effectively the many fruits of this work.

Professor Dr Arno de Schepper
Waalre, the Netherlands

Preface

Managing projects successfully

The popularity of integrated standard software is steadily increasing. So-called enterprise resource planning (ERP) packages such as SAP R/3, Baan, and Peoplesoft are experiencing rapid worldwide growth. Some of the reasons behind this trend can be identified as follows:

- ERP software integrates various business processes and therefore allows cross-functional coordination.
- It offers a great variety of standard solutions for individual business problems. This flexibility enables companies to respond quickly to changing technologies and market demands.
- With the use of ERP packages, expensive development and mainten-ance of tailor-made ERP software can be avoided. Information technology costs can be curtailed. The millennium accelerates this trend toward ERP solutions. Many companies are being forced to replace their outdated software before the year 2000.

In spite of the increasing demand for ERP packages, most companies lack project management skills. The implementation of an ERP package is complex. Projects often fail to meet the deadline and stay within the budget. A successful implementation depends on highly specialized project management skills.

How can this book help you?

Drawing on the case study of a large-scale SAP R/3 implementation, this book offers you an insight into the various principles and techniques of a successful ERP implementation. It will help you to:

- Avoid project pitfalls.
- Organize and manage an efficient and effective project.
- Implement a project successfully.

The book not only focuses on project management in the narrow sense. It also describes pre- and post-project activities; it provides background analysis of the project framework; it explains related areas such as risk management, business process re-engineering, and change management; and it offers a detailed insight into the critical success factors, objectives, strategy, costs, and throughput time of the project.

The content is structured for easy reference, with each project phase systematically described and the lessons learned clearly summarized.

The great advantage of this book is its practical approach. The helpful hints, lessons learned, critical success factors, and the tools and strategies derived from this case study can be easily and successfully applied to any project.

Who should read this book?

Our target readers include all decision-makers, project managers, project leaders, project members and professional trainers within companies implementing ERP packages. Yet the book also offers practical guidelines for project management in general.

As a case study of the wide-ranging implementation of an integrated standard software package in a multi-site environment, it may also appeal to those following university-level courses in finance, logistics, and operations.

Norbert Welti

Contents

Foreword   vii

Preface   ix

1   Case study background   1

    1.1   Company profile   1
        1.1.1   General information   1
        1.1.2   Products   2

    1.2   The enterprise resource planning package SAP R/3   3

2   The project framework   5

    2.1   Project life cycle and project phases   5

    2.2   Implementation strategy   7
        2.2.1   Step-by-step implementation   7
        2.2.2   Big bang implementation   8
        2.2.3   Roll-out   9
        2.2.4   Our project implementation approach   10

    2.3   Special characteristics of the project   11
        2.3.1   Multi-site environment   11
        2.3.2   Inter-company projects   12
        2.3.3   Internationalization   12
        2.3.4   Complexity of the project   13

    2.4   Lessons learned for project framework   14

3   Initiating phase   15

4   Planning phase   17

    4.1   Project scope   17
        4.1.1   Project definition   17

	4.1.2	Project objectives	18
		Measurements of success	18
		Definition of objectives	18
	4.1.3	Project strategy	20
		Defining the project strategy	20
	4.1.4	Lessons learned for project scope	21

4.2 Project organization 21

	4.2.1	Awkward project organization	21
	4.2.2	Efficient project organization	22
	4.2.3	Lessons learned for project organization	24

4.3 Project resources 24

	4.3.1	Human resources	25
		Provision of human resources	25
		Human resources in a project	25
		Human resources participation	26
		Trust	27
		Incentives for project members	28
		Steering committee	29
		Project manager	30
		Project secretary	33
		Project management team	34
		Project team	34
		Information technology team	35
	4.3.2	Consulting	36
		Consultant evaluation	36
		Tasks and responsibilities of a consultant	37
		Consulting company	37
		Consultancy pricing	38
		Internal consulting	39
	4.3.3	Cost	40
		Budgeting external costs	40
		Internal costs	43
		Estimating budgeted cost	44
	4.3.4	Lessons learned for project resources	44

4.4 Project administration 46

	4.4.1	Reporting	46
		Weekly reporting	46
		Progress reporting	49
	4.4.2	Time recording	49
	4.4.3	Meeting management techniques	50
		Meetings as a fundamental part of project work	50
		Meeting agenda	50

		Tips for the preparation of a meeting	52
		Essential etiquette for meetings	52
		Minutes	53
		Project team meetings	54
	4.4.4	Information and communication	54
		Project marketing	54
		Project bulletin	54
	4.4.5	Project facilities	55
	4.4.6	Project standards	56
		Purpose of standards	56
		Definition of standards	56
	4.4.7	Project handbook	56
	4.4.8	Lessons learned for project administration	56
4.5	**Project implementation plan**		**58**
	4.5.1	Creation of an implementation schedule	58
	4.5.2	Project management software	59
	4.5.3	Lessons learned for project implementation plan	61
4.6	**Concepts**		**61**
	4.6.1	As-is concept	62
		Description of content	62
	4.6.2	To-be concept	63
		Purpose of the to-be concept	63
		Software guidelines for the to-be concept	64
		Responsibility for the to-be concept	65
		Description of content	65
		Consequences of the to-be concept	68
	4.6.3	Lessons learned for concepts	68
4.7	**Technical environment**		**69**
	4.7.1	Hardware	70
		SAP server	70
		WAN	71
	4.7.2	Software	72
		Software purchase	72
		Programming guidelines	72
	4.7.3	Maintenance of hardware and software	74
	4.7.4	Lessons learned in the technical environment	74
5	**Realization phase**		**75**
5.1	**Model organizational structure**		**75**
5.2	**Customizing**		**76**

5.3	**Conversion and interfaces**		**76**
	5.3.1	Considerations for conversion and interfaces	76
	5.3.2	Conversion and interface project	77
	5.3.3	Conversion and interface handbook	78
5.4	**Forms and reports**		**78**
	5.4.1	Forms	78
		Customizing	79
		Programming the form	79
		Print output	79
	5.4.2	Reports	79
		Reporting needs	79
		Report-request form	80
5.5	**Authorization**		**80**
5.6	**Prototyping**		**81**
5.7	**Lessons learned for realization phase**		**81**

6	**Preparation phase**		**83**
6.1	**User manual and support**		**83**
	6.1.1	User manual	83
	6.1.2	User support	84
6.2	**Archiving**		**84**
	6.2.1	Archiving tool	84
	6.2.2	On-line availability of data	85
6.3	**Integration test**		**86**
6.4	**Data transfer**		**86**
6.5	**Going live preparation**		**86**
	6.5.1	Start date	86
	6.5.2	Project member preparation	87
	6.5.3	Technical preparation	87
		Hardware preparation	87
		Software preparation	88
6.6	**Lessons learned for preparation phase**		**88**

7	**Productive phase**		**90**
7.1	**Optimize system**		**90**
7.2	**Business process re-engineering (BPR)**		**91**
	7.2.1	BPR after project implementation	91
	7.2.2	Elements of business management	92

7.2.3   Business process re-engineering projects   93
        Project 1: Define customer matrix   94
        Project 2: Define performance measurements   95
        Project 3: Reduce amount of self-collectors   96
        Project 4: Clarify definition of functions and tasks 96
        *Project 5: Set up activity plan for lead-time
            reduction*   96
        Project 6: Investigate allocation policy   96
        Project 7: Decrease stock   97
        Project 8: Reduce start-up losses   97
        Project 9: Decrease number of cores   98
        Project 10: Planning for foaming and cross-linking 98
        *Project 11: Investigate and improve supply-chain
            management*   99
        Project 12: Evaluate process for small orders   99

7.3   **Follow-up projects**   99

7.4   **Lessons learned for the productive phase**   101

8   **Overall project phases**   102

8.1   **Training**   102
        8.1.1   Training of users   102
        8.1.2   Training of steering committee members   103
        8.1.3   Training of project members   103
                System-specific training   103
                Line-specific training   104
                Project-management-specific training   104
        8.1.4   Internal versus external training   104
        8.1.5   Lessons learned for training   105

8.2   **Project control**   106
        8.2.1   Project-controlling cycle   106
                Defining   106
                Measuring   107
                Correcting   107
                Coaching   108
        8.2.2   Organization of project control   108
                Internal control   108
                External control   108
                Issue list   108
        8.2.3   Monitoring   109
                Implementation schedule   110
                Meetings   110
                Reporting   110

8.2.4 Time control   111
8.2.5 Lessons learned for project control   111

8.3   **Risk management**   **112**
8.3.1 Risk identification   112
8.3.2 Risk analysis   114
8.3.3 Risk response   114
8.3.4 Reflection on risk analysis   115
8.3.5 Risk of resignation   117
8.3.6 Lessons learned for risk management   118

8.4   **Change management**   **119**
8.4.1 Preparation for change   119
8.4.2 Change perceived as negative   119
8.4.3 Change perceived as positive   121
8.4.4 Coping with change   122
8.4.5 Conclusion   124
8.4.6 Lessons learned for change management   124

9   **Closing phase**   **126**
9.1   **Project analysis and documentation**   **126**
9.2   **Handing over the product to the line organization** **126**
9.2.1 SAP coordination organization   127
       Organizational structure   127
       Functions in the SAP coordination organization   127
9.2.2 Tasks and responsibilities   129
       *Tasks and responsibilities of the SAP coordination
       manager*   129
       Tasks and responsibilities of the SAP coordinator 129
       *Tasks and responsibilities of the module
       coordinator*   129
       Tasks and responsibilities of the module leader   129
9.2.3 Administration of the SAP coordination
       organization   130
       Reporting   130
       Meeting pattern   130
9.3   **Reintegration of project members**   **130**
9.4   **Lessons learned from the closing phase**   **131**

10   **Special problems during project implementation**   **132**
10.1 **Material master maintenance**   **132**
10.2 **Data accuracy**   **133**

10.3 Program errors 133

10.4 Make-to-order or make-to-stock production 134

10.5 SAP program add-on 135
 10.5.1 Problem description 135
 10.5.2 General description of the add-on program 135
  Creation of a run number 135
  Change transaction 136
  Confirmation of a run number 136
  Various production reports 136

11 **Conclusions** 137

11.1 Thirteen factors for a successful implementation 137

11.2 Project analysis 140
 11.2.1 Project objectives analysis 140
  Objectives and savings per module 140
  Conclusion on project objectives 140
 11.2.2 Project strategy analysis 144
  Experience regarding the strategy 144
  Conclusion on project strategy 144
 11.2.3 Project cost/savings analysis 144
  General explanation of the cost/savings analysis
   graph 144
  Estimated and actual annual running costs 146
  Estimated and actual annual savings 147
  Annual savings less accumulated running costs 147
  Conclusion on project cost 147
 11.2.4 Project throughput time analysis 148
  Deadline principles 148
  Project implemented after deadline 148
  Projects implemented before deadline 150
  Conclusion on project throughput time 150

11.3 Non-financial benefits 151

11.4 Overall conclusion 152

Appendix: Documents 155

A.1 Detailed project organization 156
A.2 Project leaders' report form 157
A.3 Project members' report form 158
A.4 Report summary 159
A.5 Meeting agenda 160

A.6   Progress reporting   162

A.7   Minutes, project management team handling   163

A.8   FuturA Bulletin   164

A.9   Detailed implementation schedule   166

A.10 Authorization request form   172

A.11 Test procedure for migration   174

A.12 Time schedule for migration   176

Index   **179**

Trademark notice
ALVEOLEN, ALVEOLIT and ALVEOLUX are registered trademarks of
ALVEO AG; IXOS is a trademark of iXOS Software GmbH; Microsoft Excel,
Microsoft Project and Windows NT are trademarks of Microsoft
Corporation; Oracle is a trademark of Oracle Corporation; Peoplesoft is a
registered trademark of Peoplesoft; UNIX is a registered trademark,
licensed through X/OPEN Company Ltd. SAP® is a registered trademark
of SAP Aktiengesellschaft, Systems, Applications and Products in Data
Processing, Neurottstrasse 16, 69190 Walldorf, Germany.
The publisher gratefully acknowledges SAP's kind permission to use its
trademark in this publication. SAP AG is not the publisher of this book
and is not responsible for it under any aspect of press law.

1 Case study background

1.1 Company profile

This book is based around a case study of a large-scale SAP R/3 implementation.

As a background to the case study, first we must briefly introduce the ALVEO company featured.

1.1.1 General information

ALVEO specializes in the marketing, sales, production, and development of polyolefin foams, and aims at being market leader in this field. Its organizational structure is decentralized but close knit.

ALVEO was founded in 1971 as a joint venture company with Swiss, Japanese, and American partners. Since 1973 Sekisui Chemicals has controlled 100% of the company. ALVEO has three sister companies with approximately 400 employees.

The European headquarters for the foam operation is located in Lucerne, Switzerland. ALVEO has two production units, one in the Netherlands and the other in Wales, as well as decentralized sales offices in all key European markets. This allows the company to work closely with the local market and provide a customer- and market-specific service.

ALVEO has a turnover of more than 130 million Swiss francs (SFr). This corresponds to an annual production output of over 10000 tons (1998 figures).

To improve customer service and boost sales, ALVEO has divided the market into three sectors:

1. **Consumer/industrial sector**
    *   Sports and leisure: e.g. camping and gymnastic mats, body protection, helmet lining.
    *   Consumer items: e.g. point of sale displays, promotional articles, toys.
    *   Shoe industry: e.g. sports shoe innersoles, ski boot padding, slipper linings.
    *   Building and construction industry: e.g. floor underlay and floating floor constructions, eaves filler profiles, tube and pipe insulation, road and bridge expansion joints, flexible fillers and concrete curing covers.

- Appliance industry: e.g. sealing gaskets, insulation, and anti-vibration materials.
- Buoyancy: e.g. floating oil hoses and booms, life jackets, buoys, ship fenders, and a variety of buoyancy and swimming aids.
- Packaging: a variety of applications including cushion packaging, case inserts, and display items.

2. **Transportation sector**
   - Automotive industry: e.g. door panels, headrests, upholstery, sun visors, carpet backing, trunk compartment lining.

3. **Specialized sector**
   - Adhesive tapes: used as a supportive carrier for single- and double-sided tapes in automotive, construction, and DIY applications.
   - Medical applications: used for ECG and electro-surgical pads, dental aids, and orthopaedic splints and supports.

1.1.2　Products

ALVEO operates three fundamentally different manufacturing technologies, and offers the most comprehensive range of products. This encourages customers to adopt the principle of single-source supply. Many varied polyolefin resins are used in the manufacture of ALVEO products to meet the requirements of different industries. The foam is soft and pliable, resistant to high temperatures, with special vacuum-forming properties. It can fulfill other special requirements such as flame retardancy and electrical conductivity.

The following two products are closed-cell, physically cross-linked polyolefin foams in continuous sheets with two process skins:

- **ALVEOLIT**　Produced in densities of 25–$250 \, kg/m^3$. The sheet thickness ranges from 0.5 to 6 mm, and the width is up to 2 m depending on the density.
- **ALVEOLEN**　Produced in densities of 28–$167 \, kg/m^3$. The sheet thickness ranges from 4 to 12 mm, and the width is up to 2.5 m depending on the density.

The thickness range can be expanded for both products by laminating different foams.

The next product is a chemically cross-linked polyolefin foam produced in a broad range of colours.

- **ALVEOLUX**　A closed-cell foam, produced in dimensions of up to 1×2 m with a net useable thickness of up to 85 mm depending on the density, which ranges from 30 to $200 \, kg/m^3$.

In-depth company information is published on the ALVEO Internet home page www.alveo.com.

1.2 The enterprise resource planning package SAP R/3

Every company needs dynamic strategies to meet the challenges of today's fast-paced business world. It is crucial for a company to respond flexibly to new customer demands, and to seize market opportunities as they arise. A powerful, flexible and open IT infrastructure is needed to provide optimal support for the business, and to respond rapidly to change. SAP is the leading global provider of client/server business application solutions. Its R/3 standard business software for client/server computing provides ideal support for all business processes. The components of the R/3 system are characterized by a high degree of functionality. The high level of integration in the individual applications guarantees data consistency throughout the system and the company itself.

SAP R/3 pursues a flexible and modular structure of individual components (Figure 1.1). These individual components are as follows.

- Basic system:
  - basic components (BC)
  - advanced business application programming (ABAP/4).

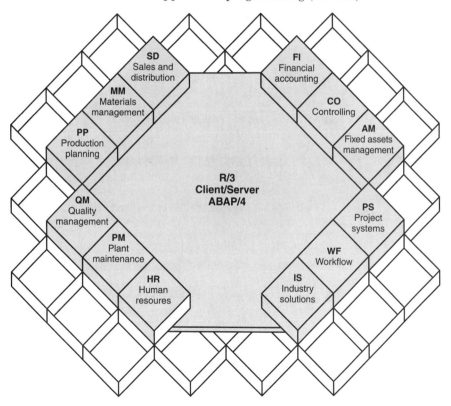

Figure 1.1 SAP R/3 modules.

- Accounting system:
  - financial accounting (FI)
  - controlling (CO)
  - asset management (AM).
- Production and logistics:
  - sales and distribution (SD)
  - materials management (MM)
  - production planning (PP)
  - quality management (QM)
  - plant maintenance (PM).
- Others:
  - project system (PS)
  - human resources (HR)
  - workflow (WF)
  - industry solutions (IS).

Detailed information about SAP can be found on the SAP Internet home page www.sap.com.

2. The project framework

Our projects were pursued in a complex environment, which demands more than just project management. This chapter provides a basic structure for understanding the context in which the projects were implemented.

2.1 Project life cycle and project phases

The project life cycle defines the beginning and end of a project, and identifies its different phases. We looked at various standard project life cycles when introducing our SAP projects. There were always several points that did not match our project management concept. Our solution was to develop our own project life cycle specifically tailored to our needs (Figure 2.1).

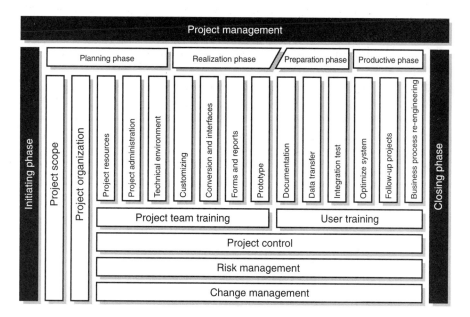

Figure 2.1   Project life cycle.

The four major phases are:

1. Planning phase (see Chapter 4).
2. Realization phase (see Chapter 5).
3. Preparation phase (see Chapter 6).
4. Productive phase (see Chapter 7).

The following overall project activities were not integrated into any particular phase as they were ongoing during the whole project:

*   Training (see Section 8.1).
*   Project control (see Section 8.2).
*   Risk management (see Section 8.3).
*   Change management (see Section 8.4).

This book follows the phases of this project life cycle chronologically, beginning with the initiating phase (Chapter 3) and ending with the closing phase (Chapter 9). The initiating and closing phases frame the project life cycle. The initiating phase evaluates the software and hardware; the closing phase terminates the project by analyzing and documenting the outcome, and formalizing the acceptance of the project by the line organization.

The organization of the four major phases was as follows:

1. **Planning phase** (Chapter 4)   This was the basis for the entire project. All planning and organizational matters were designed to enable fast progress in the subsequent phases. The scope of the project was defined, the organization assembled, the resources allocated, detailed activities planned, concepts established, and the technical environment set up. The planning phase should be completely finished before proceeding with the realization phase.
2. **Realization phase** (Chapter 5)   During this phase a system prototype was built up to reflect all the company processes and procedures defined in the to-be concept (see Section 4.6). The main activities in this phase were the customizing of the system (configuring all system tables) according to your needs; creating reports and forms required by the company; building the conversion and interface programs; and setting up the authorizations. The realization and preparation phases overlap, in that certain activities from the preparation phase may start during the realization phase.
3. **Preparation phase** (Chapter 6)   This phase anticipated the start of production and the handover to the line organization. The production system was customized, integration and quality tests were carried out in the production environment, and finally the production data was transferred from the old to the new system. User documentation was produced, and the users had to be well prepared and trained for the changeover.

4. **Productive phase** (Chapter 7)   The line organization had to take over ownership of and responsibility for the implemented system. The project team had to fine-tune the system and wind up the project by listing its achievements.

Training, project control, risk management, and change management are ongoing throughout all project phases.

- **Training** (see Section 8.1)   Training starts with the education of the project team in system, line, and project management, and ends with the training of the users.
- **Project control** (see Section 8.2)   Project control should be carried out during the whole project, following the project control cycle. The project team must identify and continually measure deviations from the project schedule.
- **Risk management** (see Section 8.3)   Potential risks must be identified at an early stage, and thoroughly analyzed, and appropriate preventive measures must be initiated to avoid the risks identified.
- **Change management** (see Section 8.4)   Users may perceive changes either positively or negatively. These change cycles must be actively managed by the respective project leader.

2.2 Implementation strategy

A fundamental decision must be taken as to the implementation strategy: step-by-step, big bang or roll-out. With the step-by-step approach the modules are implemented consecutively, while with the big bang approach all modules are implemented simultaneously. The roll-out approach creates a model implementation at one site, which is then rolled out to other sites.

Aspects such as organizational structure, resources, attitude toward change, or distance between the various production facilities may influence the company's decision.

2.2.1 Step-by-step implementation

A step-by-step implementation is characterized by the implementation of the software in small steps, and normally concentrates on the implementation of a few related modules at one time. The risk of failure is relatively low, even though interfaces have to be built between the new and existing systems. These temporary interfaces are time consuming and costly to build, and do not really contribute to the quality of the end result. The total project throughput time is lengthened. Before adopting this approach, an overall concept must be established for all relevant business processes in order to avoid difficulties in later implementations.

Opportunities arising from a step-by-step implementation:

- There is reduced complexity for coordinating, controlling, and organizing the project and resources.
- A minimal amount of human resourcing is required for the project team and the user community. This enables even a medium-sized company to implement large projects.
- The quality of the projects constantly improves, because the project members increase their knowledge and skills with every project they implement.
- Internal consulting for subsequent projects is possible on the basis of the experience gained in prior projects.
- There is a smoother changeover throughout the company: people have time to adapt to changes in their working environment.
- Costs are spread over a longer period of time.
- Modest organizational changes can be considered during the implementation of the software.
- The functionality of the software can be verified and the implementation model determined accordingly. Further functions may be available in later versions.

Threats arising from a step-by-step implementation:

- There is a longer project throughput time.
- Interfaces must be customized and programmed to maintain the data transfer for unimplemented modules, and, later on, to adjust the already running modules to the newly implemented ones.
- The project members' motivation declines with such a lengthy project.
- Integration advantages of the software can only be used step-by-step.
- Previously implemented processes may need to be redesigned as new knowledge is gained with each additional component.
- Customizing may not be optimally set because integrating components have not yet been implemented.

2.2.2 Big bang implementation

A big bang implementation replaces existing systems in a single operation with the new enterprise software. This approach is useful for companies with a straightforward organizational structure. It requires an intensive testing phase to check all business processes in detail.

Opportunities arising from a big bang approach:

- Few or even no interfaces between the old system and the new application are needed because all modules go into production at the same time.
- There is a short throughput time.

- The integrated system functions may be used immediately.
- The project members' motivation is high.
- It is highly efficient, because redundant customizing is avoided.
- There is optimal integration of all components under consideration of the integrated business processes.

Threats arising from a big bang approach:

- The implementation is complex owing to the increased need for coordination and integration.
- It is resource intensive (in financial and human resources) over a short period of time.
- All employees are subject to higher stress levels at the same time.
- A high degree of consultant support is necessary during the implementation.
- Top management needs to be closely involved, and must respond rapidly to issues regarding changes and integration of the various business processes in the organization.
- Organizational changes must be limited so as not to overwhelm employees.
- In order to reduce complexity, only modest project objectives can be set.
- Quality of data and data conversions must be flawless if a disaster is to be avoided.

2.2.3 Roll-out

The roll-out approach creates a model implementation at one site, which is then rolled out to other sites. The roll-out itself may be implemented as a big bang or a step-by-step implementation, with the opportunities and threats listed above. The roll-out implementation offers the following additional opportunities:

- There is experience gained by project members involved in the model implementation.
- Expertise is available for a fast implementation.
- Costs are kept low because only limited resources are needed.
- Risks are reduced because most problems have already been solved in the model implementation.
- There is uniformity in all company sites.
- Mutual understanding increases among the various sites.

... and these specific threats:

- Customization must also consider company standards in the subsequent implementations.
- Some site-specific processes could be overlooked.

2.2.4 Our project implementation approach

We opted for a step-by-step implementation and roll-out from one plant to the other. The main reasons in our case were limited resources and the lack of specific software functionality, especially in the PP environment. Furthermore we wanted to limit the complexity.

The roll-out from the Netherlands plant to the UK plant saved us enormous costs, human resources and time. We did not achieve our aim of total uniformity for both plants. Although the company manufactures the same product in both plants, there are still minor differences in certain processes because of the different size of the plants.

Over a period of three years we implemented all our SAP modules on schedule and within budget at the headquarters, the sales offices, and the Netherlands and UK plants (Table 2.1).

Table 2.1 Project implementation overview

Module		Year 1	Year 2	Year 3	Year 4
	Headquarters and sales				
SD	Sales and distribution	■			
	Budgeting		■		
	Sales information system				
	SD follow-up projects			■	■
FI	Finance Lucerne	■			
	Finance sales offices		■		
CO	Profit analysis			■	
	Netherlands plant				
FI	Finance	■			
CO	Cost center accounting		■		
	Product costing			■	
	Profit analysis			■	
AM	Asset management		■		
MM	Material management	■			
WM	Warehouse management	■			
	Purchasing		■		
PP	Production planning		■		
PM	Plant maintenance		■		
	Follow-up projects			■	
HR	Human resources				■
	UK plant				
FI	Finance	■			
CO	Cost center accounting			■	
	Product costing			■	
	Profit analysis			■	
AM	Asset management				
MM	Material management	■			
	Purchasing			■	
PP	Production planning			■	
PM	Plant maintenance			■	
	Follow-up projects				■

For the abbreviations used in this table please refer to Section 1.2.

During the first year we completed the first phase of our SAP project by implementing the sales and distribution (SD) module at all sales offices in Europe; the finance (FI) modules at the headquarters and both plants; the material management (MM) and warehouse management (WM) module at the Netherlands plant and the material management (MM) at the UK plant.

In the second year we implemented FI at all sales offices; the cost center accounting part (CO-CCA) of the costing module, assets management (AM), purchasing (MM-PUR) and plant maintenance (PM) at the Netherlands plant.

In the third year we implemented profit analysis (CO-PA) at the headquarters and rolled it out to the Netherlands plant and the UK plant. We finished production planning (PP) and another part of the costing module, namely product costing (CO-PC), at the Netherlands plant. Furthermore, we carried out the roll-out to the UK plant with the implementation of PM, MM-PUR, PP, CO-PC, CO-CCA, and AM.

After introducing all major modules, we focused on the improvement of every module with some 30 follow-up projects and the human resources (HR) module in the Netherlands plant.

2.3 Special characteristics of the project

The special characteristics of our SAP project were its multi-site environment, inter-company projects, internationalization, and the complexity arising from this. These circumstances had to be considered over the whole project.

2.3.1 Multi–site environment

ALVEO's organizational infrastructure, with one production facility in the Netherlands and another in Wales, and with decentralized sales offices in all key European markets, created a multi-site environment for the project implementation. This factor complicated our project in the following areas:

- **Communication** Good long-distance communication required a well-developed communication network.
- **Project management** Leadership needed to be particularly strong to cope with the complexities of a multi-site implementation.
- **Cost** Additional running and investment costs were incurred for communication and hardware.
- **Human resources** More personnel were needed because the system had to be maintained at every location.
- **Hardware** This had to be sufficiently powerful to enable good response times at all sites.
- **Internationalization** The various constraints mentioned in Section 2.3.3 had to be taken into account.
- **Consulting** Organizing consultants was difficult as appropriate people were needed in each country.

2.3.2   Inter-company projects

For a few implemented SAP modules we formed joint projects, so-called inter-company projects, where people from both plants were involved and the projects done together. Other projects were carried out intra-company – that is, plant-internally – and then rolled out to the other plants. We found that both ways had their advantages and disadvantages.

Advantages of inter-company projects (are disadvantages for the intra-company project and vice versa):

- Better outcome from a wider knowledge and expertise base.
- Coordinated set-up of the system.
- Same philosophy followed.
- Increased mutual understanding between the respective plants.

Advantages of intra-company projects:

- Increased efficiency from the absence of imported philosophies and arguments.
- Faster throughput time for the project.
- Less traveling.
- Easier communication.
- Plant-specific solutions given as no compromises need to be effected.

2.3.3   Internationalization

As ALVEO is an internationally constituted company, various nationalities were represented in its project teams. This international environment created some additional complications, which needed to be considered at the outset of the project. The following issues should be taken into account in this regard.

- **Communication**   Without doubt, this is the most challenging and difficult part of any project. In our experience, the main difficulties arose not so much from language, but from the distances involved. People simply forgot to keep each other informed, or just assumed that certain people did not need particular information. To avoid such communication breakdowns, a very open information policy should be adopted for the project. A good e-mail system can help to promote this policy, but not everything can be taken care of by e-mail. Particularly serious problems need to be discussed by telephone or, preferably, face to face. An appropriate meeting schedule must be followed to maintain the necessary flow of information.
- **Differences in culture and mentality**   The culture and mentality not only differs from country to country, but also from department to department. It takes tolerance and intensive communication from both sides to reconcile differing points of view and find a solution acceptable to all concerned.

- **National and regional holidays** National and regional holidays should be respected when planning meetings, and should be taken into account when creating the implementation schedule. People need their holidays, especially during a long project.
- **Time-zone differences** Our computer hardware is located in Switzerland, and has to serve the whole of Europe. For system maintenance or system closing we always had to take into consideration the time difference between the UK and Europe and the different working hours in the sales offices and plants, especially where weekend work was involved.
- **Increased traveling** Close communication requires face-to-face contact. Since project leaders' meetings must be held at least every two weeks, this involves a lot of traveling.

2.3.4 Complexity of the project

The implementation of an integrated standard software package in an international, multi-site environment is highly complex. We experienced this complexity in the following areas:

- The wide variety and variability of the integrated standard software, once all SAP modules had been implemented.
- The relationship and interdependence of the various business units within the integrated software.
- The highly specialized software expertise required.
- The need to develop special add-on programs.
- The difficulty of modeling the company's organization and processes to correspond with the software.
- The international cultural and regulatory constraints of implementation in several different countries.
- The overlapping multi-site implementation.
- The multiple objectives of the project.
- The major extent of the information technology changes within the company.
- The changes in corporate philosophy involved in adapting the company's processes, procedures and organization to the software standards and not vice versa.
- The planning of a three-year project.

We tried to reduce the complexity of the integrated standard software package by the following means:

- A step-by-step implementation and roll-out.
- A structured approach, defining the project life cycle in its appropriate phases.

- An active involvement of top management to speed up decision-making and overcome political obstacles.
- Clear, concise and well-focused project objectives.
- Simple, streamlined organizational structures.
- Clearly defined and allocated tasks and responsibilities.
- Strict adherence to deadlines.
- A high standard of external consultancy.
- Well-qualified project management and project members.
- Tight project control.
- A reliable software supplier.
- A safe technical environment.
- Business process re-engineering after software implementation.

Reducing complexity in the project is one step toward achieving success. Another is adopting the flexibility to respond rapidly to changes arising out of the project. The company must adapt itself to the software, expand its skills base, and fully exploit the expertise it has acquired. In this, flexibility and corporate culture will play a key role.

2.4 Lessons learned for project framework

1. **Adopt the right implementation strategy** The implementation strategy must be carefully selected according to the particular constraints of the company. Such constraints may include the availability of human resources, of specialized expertise, of financial resources, and of time. The strategy adopted will have an impact on the project objectives, on the throughput time, on the project costs, on the use of external consultants, on the degree of complexity, on the quality of the implementation, and on the company organization itself.

2. **Consider international differences** An international environment creates additional complications arising from different cultures, conflicting holidays, communication difficulties, time differences, etc. All of these need to be considered when setting up and implementing the project.

3. **Reduce complexity** The implementation of an integrated standard software package in an international, multi-site environment is highly complex. This complexity has to be reduced by carefully structuring the project, by securing top management support, by providing clear project objectives, by using skilled external consultants, by recruiting well-qualified project management and members, by keeping project control tight, and by employing reliable software (refer to the project success factors in Section 11.1).

3 Initiating phase

The ALVEO company decided to replace its outdated computer system in all business areas with new software and appropriate hardware. The initiating phase to evaluate new hardware and software had to be finished within four months to be able to start the planning phase at the beginning of the following year. The SAP implementation project was called FuturA, standing for 'The *Futur*e of *A*LVEO.'

A totally new IT environment was desperately needed at ALVEO on the following grounds:

- **Information need** Detailed information concerning processes and products was needed as a basis for management decisions.
- **Cost transparency** Better production cost transparency was necessary to improve the quality of decisions.
- **Customer service** The available software could not comply with the increasing demands from customers for faster and reliable responses to inquiries and shorter delivery times.
- **Competition** Flexible and integrated software was needed to keep up with competitors.
- **On-line access** On-line access to various data, especially stock and production data, was required.
- **Simpler administration** Administrative processes had to be facilitated.
- **Internal communication** An IT infrastructure was needed for fast and efficient communication within the international organization.
- **External communication** Preparation for electronic communication with our customers and suppliers.
- **Millennium problem** The old IT environment was not year 2000 compliant and therefore was a potential risk.
- **Company growth** ALVEO was in need of software suitable for a growing international company.

Up to that time there were only about three software suppliers offering a suitable enterprise resource planning package. The prospective software had to overcome the disadvantages of the existing software mentioned above, and fulfill the following additional requirements:

- Functionality to cover ALVEO's business processes.

- Integration of all business processes.
- Adaptability to changing environment.
- Multilingual facilities.
- Covering international standards and requirements.
- Standard software.
- Reliable software supplier.

After having examined all three of them, ALVEO came to the conclusion that SAP R/3 suited its needs best. In addition, SAP was already some kind of an industry standard, which was also a certain guarantee for continuity.

4 Planning phase

The first phase in the project life cycle – the planning phase – is the basis for the entire project. The project is organized and planned to enable fast progress in the subsequent phases. In this phase the project scope is defined, the organization enrolled, the resources allocated, the implementation schedule created, the as-is and to-be concepts established, and the technical environment set up.

The planning phase should be completely finished before starting the realization phase. If the objectives and especially the as-is and to-be concepts are not thoroughly discussed and described before starting the realization phase, unnecessary delays may occur for the following reasons:

- Necessary decisions are not taken by the management. This hinders the project team from working continuously on the project.
- If important decisions are not recorded, for example in the to-be concept or the project handbook, particular decisions will be debated over and over again because people tend to forget what they said a few months ago.
- The project team has to justify and explain its work constantly, which is, of course, very time consuming.

4.1 Project scope

The project scope includes the project definition, objectives, and strategy. All these components of the project scope are necessary to create a clear project vision that everybody can understand and follow. People need a sense of vision both during and after the project.

4.1.1 Project definition

The project definition explains in a brief yet comprehensive way the idea of the project. It gives an answer to the question: what is the purpose of the project?

The project definition should not contain any specific goals or strategies. An example is shown in Table 4.1.

Table 4.1 Project definition

ALVEO wants to replace its outdated computer system with a new
operation-wide IT system serving accounting, sales, production, and logistics
functions. A wide area network has to ensure the electronic link among all
units of ALVEO operations. **FuturA**: 'The Future of ALVEO' is the project we
have commissioned to implement this change.

4.1.2   Project objectives

Measurements of success

In our experience, well-defined objectives help to keep the project team
focused on the aim of the project. They are essential for measuring progress.

We therefore considered well-defined project objectives as a crucial
success factor for every project. The project objectives should be:

- clearly defined
- simple yet comprehensive
- measurable
- controllable
- clear in regard to estimated savings
- realistic but still challenging.

The objectives must be coordinated with other projects. After project
implementation, the objectives have to be verified. Most project objectives
may only be measured after project implementation because they ask for
results based on the implementation, or aim for organizational changes.

Wherever possible the savings targets should be calculated. This may be
time consuming, but it is well worth the effort to prove the profitability of
the project.

The objectives for the overall project have to be set by the highest
authority of the project organization: the steering committee (see
Section 4.3). The objectives for every individual project have to be defined
by the project teams. Table 4.2 shows the targets we have set for our SAP
project. Certain targets do not indicate any savings because they were not
easily measurable in financial terms. In Section 11.2.1 the objectives
mentioned in Table 4.2 have been analyzed, and conclusions are drawn.

Definition of objectives

The steering committee must define the objectives for the program, and the
line managers are responsible for the objectives of those projects that
concern their departments. The involvement of the management in the
definition of the project objectives is already a first step toward management ownership of the project.

Table 4.2 SAP project objectives

Module	Target	Control method	Expected annual savings (in SFr)
SD	1. To ensure that response time on inquiries will be below 2 hours	Random check with local sales organizations and their customers	
	2. To ensure reliability of answers to customers	Random check with local sales organizations and their customers	
	3. To optimize routine administration work in sales	• Savings: SFr40,000 • Marginal profit: SFr60,000	40,000 60,000
	4. To improve balance between customer requirements and material availability	• Stock reduction • Compliance with rules of demand/supply system	
FI	5. To reduce average payment terms by 5 days	Reduction of days outstanding from 75 to 70 days	40,000
	6. To optimize routine administration work in finance	Savings: SFr40,000	40,000
PP/MM	7. To reduce throughput time 50% (order planning and production)	From 10 to 5 working days	
	8. To achieve stock reduction of 40%	Reduce stock (value 5 million) by 40%	580,000
	9. To increase stock turnover from 12 to 24	Check stock figures	370,000
	10. To improve operation ratio by 1%	Saving by better planning and shop floor scheduling	600,000
	11. To improve yield by 0.5%	Saving by better planning and shop floor scheduling	300,000
All	12. To increase overall output by 2.5% with the same number of staff	Annual savings = 8 persons = 8 × SFr60,000	500,000
	Estimated total savings		**2,530,000**

It pays to spend time in defining project objectives carefully, since the more clearly they are formulated the more precisely you can estimate savings and analyze results.

People tend to promise too much in a project. They forget that a project will be judged on whether the deadlines were met and the goals achieved. After the project implementation nobody will be concerned about what it cost or the amount of consultant input it required.

In short, success depends on the management of expectations.

When it comes to identifying objectives, the project manager can contribute in the following ways:

- By relating objectives to the company business plan.
- By clarifying and communicating them to all the managers.
- By highlighting the potential benefits and savings.
- By spreading the objectives evenly across the four elements of business management: information technology, organization, processes, methods and procedures (see Section 7.2.2).

4.1.3 Project strategy

Defining the project strategy

The project strategy sets the guidelines for the project. It needs to be defined by the steering committee and followed by all project members. Table 4.3 shows how we formulated ours.

According to Table 4.3, the project strategy should contain the following elements:

- project locations
- departments involved
- implementation philosophy
- hardware and software to be used.

Above all, the company must understand that it has to adopt the philosophy of the standard software. This means adapting the company organization, its processes, and procedures to the software standard – and not vice versa!

The project strategy has been analyzed in Chapter 11.

Table 4.3 Project strategy

For the implementation of the SAP system, the steering committee has approved the following project strategy:

1. We intend to implement the SAP R/3 system for all our affiliates in Europe to serve accounting, controlling, sales, production, and logistics.
2. We shall adopt a step-by-step and roll-out approach, introducing the different modules at each site throughout Europe.
3. Deadlines established in the implementation schedules are to be met at all costs.
4. The project is to be implemented by our own staff. Consultancy should be kept to a minimum, and project members should be trained up as appropriate.
5. Major focus is to be put on management support at all levels.
6. We plan to implement the SAP R/3 software without modifications to its source. We shall adapt and standardize our organization, processes, and procedures in accordance with the standard software SAP R/3. Any change to the SAP R/3 software will require approval by the steering committee.
7. We propose the use of a central computer based in Switzerland, with the plants and sales offices being connected via a wide area network (WAN).

4.1.4   Lessons learned for project scope

1. **Define simple, clear, and measurable objectives**   Well-defined objectives help to keep the project focused on its aims, and are an essential yardstick for analyzing and measuring success. The objectives must be clear, measurable, and controllable, and must indicate the estimated savings in each case.

2. **Calculate savings for each objective**   This should be done wherever possible because it proves the cost-effectiveness of the project.

3. **Make the line manager responsible for the objectives**   It is the line managers' task to set up the objectives for the projects concerning their departments, since they need to assume ownership of the project and usually have the highest level of expertise in their departments.

4. **Put deadlines before cost**   Meeting deadlines is more important than costs. It is better to spend more money than prolong the throughput time.

5. **Adapt your organization, its processes, and procedures to the software**   The company must be made aware of the fact that adopting the philosophy of the standard software means adapting its own organization, processes, and procedures to the software standard, and not vice versa.

4.2   Project organization

We set up the project organization separately from the line organization because the implementation of integrated standard software is process oriented and covers all departments. Furthermore we wanted to ensure creativity, innovation, and short decision lines. Hence the project was embedded in the company organization as one element in a matrix organization.

We started our project with an unfavorable project organization (see Section 4.2.1), realized this mistake, and subsequently changed to a very effective and efficient model (see Section 4.2.2).

4.2.1   Awkward project organization

We started our project with the organizational structure illustrated in Figure 4.1. We realized that this kind of structure was not very efficient.

Inefficiency was rooted in the following:

- **Organizational structure**   Decision and communication lines were complicated, and were slowed down by the existence of five hierarchical levels and the corresponding allocation of responsibilities.

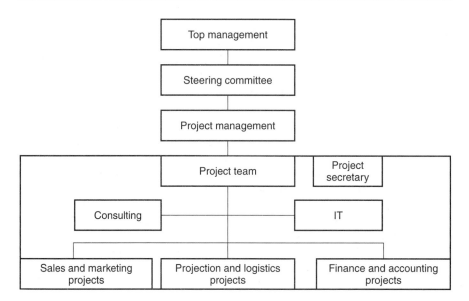

Figure 4.1   Awkward project organization.

- **No top management involvement**   The steering committee consisted of members from the middle management. We realized that it was incapable of taking decisions on organizational matters, program changes or human resources. Only top management could do this; but they were reluctant to intervene as they had little appreciation of project issues and no direct stake in the project itself. Without public backing by top managers the project lacked prestige, and was not so readily accepted.
- **An excessively large project management team**   The project team consisted of 14 members and the project management of three members. The numerous participants made meetings unwieldy and difficult to lead.

4.2.2   Efficient project organization

After about one year, we changed our organizational structure to the one shown in Figure 4.2. A detailed overview is given in the Appendix, Figure A.1.

   We set up a flat hierarchical project organization with short decision and communication lines, which proved highly efficient and effective. Tasks and responsibilities were clearly allocated among the project members (described in Section 4.3.1), and a sense of ownership was encouraged.

   The following changes were made to the organizational structure shown in Figure 4.1:

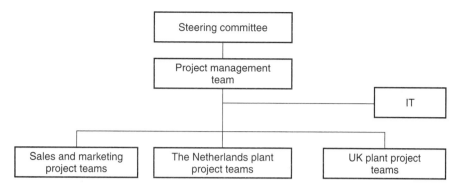

Figure 4.2 Efficient project organization.

- **Hierarchical levels**   The project levels were reduced from five to three. Level 1 was the steering committee, level 2 the project management team, and level 3 the various project teams.
- **Simplification of the structures**   After reducing the levels, the next stage was to integrate the consultants and secretaries into the project teams, and to organize the projects at each site.
- **Steering committee**   The top management became the steering committee. The project manager acted as project secretary on the steering committee, thus ensuring the link to the project team. The steering committee members were also line managers of the project team members, thus strengthening the authority of the project organization. An external management consultant coached the steering committee and the project manager.

    From that time onwards the project was taken seriously by the top management, because they had assumed ownership. An appreciation of the importance of the project was now recognized by all employees. With top managers on the steering committee, the project organization had the power necessary to drive the project through the company.
- **Project management team**   In the new project structure we merged the project team and the project management into the project management team. We reduced the team members to six, which made the meetings fruitful and efficient. The project management team consisted of the project manager, the project secretary, and several project coordinators. The project manager had the overall responsibility for the project, led the project management team, and was the linchpin between project management and the steering committee. In our case the project manager was also the IT manager, and consequently could coordinate IT with project matters. The project activities were distributed among the project coordinators. The project coordinators were responsible to the project management team for their activities.

- **Project teams** The project teams were led by the project leader, who in most cases was the line manager.
- **Information technology team** IT became a separate support unit, and as a task force it administered equally to the needs of all project levels.

4.2.3 Lessons learned for project organization

1. **Establish a flat project hierarchy with short communication lines** A flat project hierarchy works very efficiently and effectively because of its shorter decision lines, faster communication, and easier leadership. Short communication lines in the project organization enable a fast reaction to problems. Above all a fast, direct link to the steering committee chairman is essential for matters beyond the competence of the project management.
2. **Set up a separate and efficient project organization** To ensure efficiency, creativity, innovation, and short decision lines, the organizational structures of the project should be independent from the normal line organization. The steering committee is, of course, an exception.
3. **Appoint top management as the steering committee** In this way it can assume ownership, inject expertise, and empower the project. Active top management participation is crucial to provide enough resources, take fast decisions, and support the acceptance of the project throughout the company.
4. **Assign an external consultant to the project teams** An external consultant on the project team must advise on customizing, setting up the implementation schedule, and controlling the project. A consultant on the steering committee facilitates the organization, processes, and procedures, and advises the project manager on project management issues.

4.3 Project resources

The provision of resources in the appropriate quantity and quality, at the right time and at the right place, is crucial for every project. If financial or human resources (including consultants) are inadequate the project is likely to make little progress, and will eventually disintegrate. It is the steering committee's responsibility and duty to ensure correct resourcing for the project.

4.3.1   Human resources

Provision of human resources

All software implementation projects require human resources from the line organization to contribute line-specific expertise for a successful project implementation. However, engaging line workers in project work often drains departments of manpower. It is hard to convince the line managers to make their best human resources available for the project. Unfortunately they often do not appreciate that project work can be a real challenge for these people, and that subsequently there is tremendous potential benefit for the department. If recruitment problems arise the steering committee must take action.

To overcome this bottleneck in human resources, we took the following measures:

- **Hire temporary staff**   Temporary staff can take care of all the routine work in a department, thus reducing the project members' line work to only essential tasks in favor of the project.
- **Employ new people**   Employing new people is, of course, an expensive option. However, it can be seen as an opportunity to prepare staff for key positions in the department by familiarizing them with the new ways of working. A new employee always looks differently on the processes and procedures within a department, and is able to give valuable input for improvements.
- **Enlist external consultants**   An additional option is to delegate the workload to external consultants. Drawing on their experience they can speed up the project considerably. However, it is an expensive way to solve the human resources problem. The greatest disadvantage is that hardly any know-how is transferred from consultants to employees. As the know-how is not with internal people, you completely depend on external help. However, managing SAP matters through external consulting companies may also be an IT strategy. This avoids having to employ expensive SAP staff in the company.
- **Short throughput time**   A short throughput time minimizes the loss of human resources to the respective departments.

Human resources in a project

Composition of the project team

We usually structured the project teams as follows:

- **Project leader**   In most cases the project leader was a member of the line organization, preferably the line manager. In this way, line ownership of the project is guaranteed, and essential line expertise is made available to the project.

- **Project members** Project members were selected according to the skills requirements of the project. The number of project members depended on the complexity of the projects and the availability of human resources. We tried to keep the number of project members as low as possible because it is easier to lead a small group. A member of the project team is represented on every subproject to ensure the proper link to the project organization.
- **Consultant** The consultant supported the project with his experience in project planning, customizing, and training.

Quality of human resources

The quality of the project members determines the success of the project. Project work is very demanding and complex, and therefore requires people with a high learning potential. The project management team members have to be highly capable. Qualified project members ensure a fast and proper implementation. In particular, the members in the project management team have to be clever and capable, as they are the driving force of the project. The project organization is as good as its individuals.

If one of the members is weak the project can be endangered depending on the importance of that person to the project. The first corrective action should be to educate this person properly in project management, and to provide the necessary support for his or her tasks. This will almost certainly involve a lot of support from other project team members, especially from the project leader and the project manager. Another option is to replace the project member, but this is not always possible as he or she may be a specialist in a particular area.

The worst case is the failure of the project leader. In that case the project is likely to disintegrate. It is advisable to replace the project leader immediately to guarantee the success of the project. We also experienced that one of the project members was able to take over the leadership and bring the project to a successful conclusion.

Human resources participation

For every SAP project it is essential to have at least one of the project members available 'full-time' (i.e. 100% of his working hours) for the project. This ensures continuity and progress. A project with only part-time members is likely to disintegrate, since such employees tend to prioritize line work over project work. This is usually because line work is more familiar and thus the easier option. To prevent project work being treated as a secondary task the project leader must ensure deadlines are met at all costs and convince the line manager of the necessity of having his staff participating in the project.

We delineated the participation of the project members in terms of percentage per week: for example, 20% is equivalent to one day per week. The percentage used was an average for the whole duration of the project: This means that in certain phases of the project the percentage could have been more or less than agreed.

- **Project leader**   When the project leader was also a line manager, he usually dedicated 20–40% of his time to the project. He is especially needed in the first phase of the project to determine the future concept and structure of his department.
- **Project members**   The project members participated anywhere from 20 to 100%. A minimum of 20% is required, otherwise it is not a real participation in a project like the one we carried out.
- **Consultants**   Our consultants were usually 20% involved in a project. Every two weeks they were in for two days. This schedule would give the project members enough time to do their homework, investigate issues, and prepare adequately for the next meeting.

Trust

Although some project members were assigned 100% to the project, the line managers continued to be responsible for them with respect to salary, career, holiday, working hours, etc. The project manager had a limited influence on this matter. When he wanted to modify anything, he was heavily dependent first on the steering committee to enforce a change at departmental level and second on the goodwill of the line manager, on a relationship of trust. Hence the management of project members could not be based on hierarchical authority but rather on trust and natural authority.

Building up a basis of trust among the project members including the steering committee was therefore essential for the success of the project. We found that projects where the leader or the manager was not trusted or there was distrust among other project members were much more difficult to implement. These projects had to be very carefully monitored and nurtured, otherwise they went downhill fast.

Below we list some of the measures we used for building up trust:

- **Strengthening interpersonal communication**   By close personal contact among the project members with regular progress and project team meetings.

- **Increasing access to information**   With an honest and open information policy throughout the project to avoid any rumors.
- **Coaching**   Good coaching by the project manager and project leaders.
- **Allocating responsibility**   By delegating tasks and responsibility to project leaders and members to demonstrate our confidence in them.
- **Providing support**   By looking after project members in all respects, even advising them in private matters.
- **Giving incentives**   By organizing special activities for project members to strengthen team spirit or by showing appreciation with special bonuses or salary increases (see next section).

Incentives for project members

Project members deserve special treatment. They have to contribute more to the company than in normal circumstances. Through the project involvement, most of them have an exceptionally high workload, and are under intense pressure as they have to reach both line and project goals. Project work should be rewarded.

The following ideas may help to motivate the project members and create a pleasant atmosphere, promote a team spirit among them, and finally build up a basis of trust. It need not cost a lot, but the project leader or project manager should show his appreciation. Below are a few ideas for ways of acknowledging the special effort:

- Organize special events for the project members (dinner, sightseeing tour, cinema, visits, sports, etc.).
- Hold meetings away from the normal business environment.
- Verbal appreciation of the project member's work is often forgotten, but very effective.
- Nominate a project Oscar for good achievement.
- Distribute small seasonal presents (e.g. chocolate bars) to all project members.
- Publish articles and project member profiles in the project bulletin.
- To mark the successful start-up of the project organize a small presentation ceremony, where a steering committee member can present the project leader with a bottle of champagne. Photograph the event and publish it in the project bulletin.
- Acknowledge the work of steering committee members. They also need to feel appreciated.

Financial incentives should not be forgotten:

- Provide a special bonus: this may range from a small token of appreciation up to 100% of total salary for exceptional achievement.

- It is also possible to increase salary, and this, of course, would be highly appreciated by the project members, but also more difficult for the company. A rise should be at least 10%, and would be appropriate for those workers whose market value increases substantially as a result of their project work and software expertise.

Steering committee

Tasks and responsibilities

The steering committee is the top authority for a project. We considered a capable and powerful steering committee as absolutely crucial for a project, as it has to fulfill very important tasks and responsibilities:

- assuming ownership
- monitoring project targets
- managing the implementation of project policy
- controlling project planning and progress
- enabling fast decisions
- deciding on organizational issues
- making resources available
- supporting the project manager
- motivating the management
- approving proposals from the project team.

Steering committee member

To be a steering committee member is very demanding. It is not enough just to attend meetings. A steering committee member is expected to assume ownership and lead the projects under his or her responsibility.

Highly qualified and active steering committee members have an enormous impact on the project. With their active involvement they are able to keep the throughput times short and the quality of the project high, because they have the necessary authority to push the project through at all levels and to attack problems quickly and efficiently.

Our experience with top management on the steering committee was very positive, for the following reasons:

- **Fast decisions** With top management participation, the steering committee was capable of taking fast decisions for every problem in the project.
- **Decisions on structural changes** The steering committee was authorized to decide on organizational matters, and to redesign company processes and procedures.
- **Availability of resources** The steering committee was able to make sufficient resources available.

- **Project authority** With top managers participating on the steering committee, the project organization had the necessary power to push the project through the company.
- **Know-how** Top management was an invaluable source of expertise for the project.
- **Ownership** Top managers assumed ownership of the project and therefore fully identified with it.
- **Commitment** The ownership and commitment by the top management gave out a clear signal that everybody in the company had to accept this project.
- **Preventing obsolescence** Participation on the steering committee prevented the top managers from losing touch, because they were fully involved in the restructuring of processes and procedures.

Steering committee chairman

The steering committee chairman has a key position in the whole project. This individual's participation can influence the success of the project considerably.

Below are a few characteristics that we found helpful in a chairman:

- They assume ownership and lead the steering committee. The CEO often makes the best chairman.
- They are a respected and accepted authority among the steering committee members.
- They identify with the project and demonstrate their full support.
- They cooperate closely with the project manager.
- They hold regular meetings with the project manager to discuss the project progress and problems, and to prepare the steering committee meeting.
- Their door is always open to discuss relevant problems.

Project manager

The project manager has a key role in the whole project. If project managers rate badly in their tasks and responsibilities, the project is likely to fail.

Tasks and responsibilities

The project manager is the overall leader of the project. Their main task is managing, leading, and coaching. They have to make the implementation as easy as possible, and create a pleasant atmosphere and environment for the project members to work in.

The project manager should have broad authority over all elements of the project. Their authority should be sufficient to permit them to engage in all necessary managerial and technical actions required to complete the project successfully regardless of organizational barriers.

The tasks and responsibilities of the project manager are listed below:

- leading the project
- managing the project (planning, organizing, coordinating, controlling)
- coaching project members
- detecting and solving problems and conflicts
- marketing and public relations
- educating and training project leaders and steering committee
- reporting to the steering committee
- conducting quality control.

When threats to the project arise, it is the project manager's responsibility to investigate this immediately. A fast response is essential to protect the project, whatever or whoever is involved.

Skills of a project manager

Strength in the following areas is an asset for successful project management:

- **Leadership** The project manager must be assertive within the project and toward the line organization, be goal-oriented, have a sense of vision, take decisions, and motivate the project members.
- **Business management know-how** Understanding the business processes and procedures in finance, sales, and production is essential for following discussions in the various projects.
- **Organization** Organizational topics such as planning, coordinating, and controlling are daily business for a project manager.
- **Coaching** The project members must be coached and educated in their manager's special field.
- **Communication** Communicative abilities help the project manager to discuss and market the project internally and externally.
- **Risk-taking** The outcome of a project is never 100% sure. That is why a good amount of risk-taking is needed.
- **Flexibility** Circumstances in a project change quite often as new knowledge is gained and problems occur. It is normal for a project manager to deal with new situations and react accordingly.
- **Acceptance** The project manager has to be accepted by the project members, especially by the steering committee and the project management team.
- **Analytical abilities** Project management also involves a constant search for bottlenecks and problems within the projects.
- **Stress resistant** Project management is a high-pressure job.

Helpful hints for the project manager

Based on experience throughout the projects, we gathered some useful tips for the project manager:

- **Broad project overview**   The project manager has to keep an overview of the project. A broad but not necessarily very detailed knowledge about the project is required. Involvement in the detail of the project is required of the manager only in the event of problems, but in that case it should be rapid.
- **Good emotional stability**   Project management is a high-pressure job. Emotional stability is a vital factor in this job. A good balance between project involvement and private interests is desirable. The project manager should not feel guilty about taking holidays. Recreation is necessary to realize the manager's full potential and to avoid the risk of getting bogged down in project detail, becoming too emotionally involved, and losing objectivity.
- **Fair play**   Management is tough, but can still be fair and human as long as both sides play fair, giving people a second chance.
- **Acceptance and trust**   Acceptance and trust throughout the organization help the project manager to be able to market or defend the project successfully at all levels of the organization.
- **Flexible working environment**   The project manager has to travel a lot to keep track of the progress of all projects. The ability to work while on the move (whether in the airport, train or taxi) is a distinct advantage. A portable computer and a mobile phone help to achieve this goal.
- **Regular traveling schedule**   To avoid family problems, it is helpful to have a regular schedule for being away from home. The time away from home should be used for working in order to have the time back home fully available for the family.
- **Understand the mechanics of power and politics**   Influencing the organization requires an understanding of both the formal and informal structures of the organization, and the mechanics of power and politics.
- **Sparring partner**   The project manager is a solitary figure. A good sparring partner (external consultant or coach) is essential.
- **Difference between project manager and coordinator**   There are some differences between a project manager and a project coordinator. The coordinator advises and gathers the business requirements; the manager is authorized to give directives.
- **Personal contacts**   The project manager should not delegate tasks where personal contact is important (congratulations for a specific success, birthday, birth of a child, etc.).
- **Informal contacts are helpful**   It helps to take the occasional stroll through the offices or the plant and chat with the future system users to get an idea about their concerns regarding the project implementation.
- **Understand the project's environment**   It is useful for the project manager to experience the working environment where they plan to implement the software. They learn to understand departmental

processes and procedures, and the employees' problems and concerns. It is enough to be there for a day or a shift, but important is to be there.

- **Pain in the neck**   Sometimes the project manager has to be a pain in the neck, especially if projects are not working the way they should. Nevertheless, project team members find it very reassuring to know that the project manager cares about their work, and is also willing to take over responsibility.
- **No cheers for the project manager**   The project manager should expect no thanks if the project goes live without any hitch. People take it for granted.
- **Good communication**   Good communication with the steering committee chairman is important to ensure an optimal information flow and a fast reaction in case of problems.
- **Draw attention to problems in the line**   The project manager has to draw the steering committee's attention to problems in the line organization; but it is not his job to solve line problems insofar as they do not affect the project implementation itself.

Project secretary

Qualifications of a project secretary

A project secretary provides tremendous support to the project manager in areas such as administration, organization, and control.

It is important that the project secretary has the following strengths:

- **Initiative**   They must be able to work independently, as the project manager is often away and cannot dictate everything in detail.
- **Organizational flair**   A project secretary needs to be well organized, to set the right priorities and get the work done promptly and efficiently in a stressful project environment.
- **Perseverance**   The project manager may delegate to the project secretary some work such as supervising the deadlines. In order to gather the necessary information or reports from the project members, the secretary must be assertive toward them.

Tasks and responsibilities

- supporting the project manager
- organizing project administration
- supervising project reports and deadlines
- recording project time and costs
- publishing the project bulletin
- writing and archiving minutes
- organizing and planning dates, meetings, flights, accommodation, etc.

Project management team

The project management team must manage all the projects, and represent them on the steering committee. It must coordinate the various interests from all module areas, and solve those problems that cannot be solved by the project teams themselves. The project manager leads the project management team, and is the linchpin between project management and steering committee. The members of the project management team have to be 100% available for project work. They represent the programs in a business area or a module such as finance and control, sales and marketing, production, material management, and so on. They participate in all the projects within their area, but not necessarily the project leadership as this normally comes from the line side. Nevertheless, they do bear full responsibility for the proper implementation of every project they participate in.

Tasks and responsibilities

- implementing the project
- communicating, coordinating, and controlling the projects
- evaluating and deciding about functional issues
- configuring and customizing the system
- training and supporting project members and users
- documenting the project
- reporting to the project manager.

Project team

Project leader

Project leaders must have strong leadership qualities, and be familiar with the software module they are going to implement. Knowledge of the organization is an asset but not essential. A few people joined our company from outside and made successful project leaders. They were accepted by the line workers because they did a good job, and had the above-mentioned qualities.

The ideal arrangement is one where the line manager is also put in charge of the project. Line managers must participate in the project anyway, because they should be the most familiar with departmental processes and procedures, and need to understand the prospective changes within their own departments. In this way the line manager participates in the decision-making process, assumes ownership, and learns at first hand new processes and procedures. Without such involvement, line managers risk losing control as developments overtake them and they become out of touch with new processes and procedures. We found that this can happen within a relatively short time.

Project members

Project members must be fast learners, as they must absorb and apply knowledge within a short time. They must have the mental capacity to cope with the complex implementation of integrated standard software.

During the life cycle of the project, the project members must be able to concentrate on project matters rather than conflicts within the line organization: yet another reason to keep the throughput time as short as possible.

Tasks and responsibilities

- configuring and customizing the system
- working out the as-is and to-be concepts
- supporting the project management team
- training and supporting the users
- testing the system
- discussing functional issues with members of the project management
- evaluating proposals of the project management team
- reporting to the project management team.

Information technology team

Information technology (IT) function

The IT department has a service function for the whole project. Their main task is to support the project from a technical side (see Section 4.7). ALVEO's IT is organized as follows:

- **Lucerne headquarters**   Four people, consisting of the IT manager (project manager), a secretary, a systems manager, and a system application engineer.
- **Netherlands plant**   Two system application engineers, and a person responsible for each module.
- **Welsh plant**   Two system application engineers.

All the IT personnel have a dual function. On the one hand they assist with the project; on the other hand they ensure daily operation. With this limited staffing, we tried to help each other out, focusing our limited personnel on the most urgent project where IT help was needed. This task force concept is only possible in a step-by-step implementation of the modules. The IT staff at all of the sites must be trained to the same level so that work can always be allocated to whichever team may be available at any given time. To guarantee common standards, our IT training has always been organized in-house for all IT members from every location.

This task force approach has proven successful, although by no means trouble-free. Distance created communication difficulties for us. At least project members were encouraged to communicate more effectively in writing: not a bad thing in itself.

Tasks and responsibilities

- setting up and maintaining the technical infrastructure: hardware, software, LAN, WAN
- managing and controlling the infrastructure
- supporting the projects in IT matters
- analyzing and programming interfaces and conversions, documents, procedures, and reports.

4.3.2 Consulting

A great deal of know-how is essential for the complex implementation of an integrated standard software package. The success of a project depends strongly on the capabilities of the consultants because the consultant is the only one with in-depth knowledge of the software. Hence good consultants have a major impact on the throughput time and the quality of a project.

Consultant evaluation

The evaluation of a consultant or a consulting company is a matter to be taken very seriously, because consulting has such an impact on the through-put time and quality of an SAP implementation. Successful collaboration might also signal a productive relationship for the future.

We had some surprising experiences before we established a fixed procedure for recruiting consultants. We tried out a number of consultants and consulting companies. Some of them knew less than our own people; others simply gave us bad advice.

One basis system consultant recommended that we make a copy of the standard SAP client, and use the newly created client. Unfortunately not all of the tables were properly copied from the standard SAP client. This missing data caused us countless headaches during later implementations.

Other consultants would sit all day in front of screens, customizing like crazy without ever explaining a thing to our people about what they had been doing. No knowledge transfer took place, and our people were left frustrated.

Such experiences led us to establish a two-stage procedure for evaluating consultants. First, the project manager arranged a meeting with the representative of the consulting company to find out more about the quality of the company, the experience and availability of the consultants, and the pricing and conditions.

The second stage was to set up a meeting with the designated consultant and the project team members. The project team members should be involved in the recruitment process, as they must work closely with that person afterwards. We judged consultants on the following criteria:

- mutual understanding and trust
- competence and experience
- personality (capable of consensus, not stubborn, etc.)
- ready availability in the event of problems
- analytical capacity to understand company processes and procedures
- easy grasp of problems.

After approval from the management and project members, the consultant could be hired.

Tasks and responsibilities of a consultant

- meeting deadlines
- consulting, supporting, and training project group
- creating, monitoring, and verifying implementation schedule
- solving problems with specialists from SAP and the consulting company
- configuring and customizing the system
- providing quality assurance of the features implemented
- documenting all activities.

It was important for us to have a consultant who was able to transfer the necessary knowledge to our own people. We were also keen on getting the consultant to participate in the planning phase. Helping to organize the implementation schedule, consultants would take a stake in the ownership of the project. By the same token they would feel responsible for the quality of the implementation, and, of course, for the deadline. Another significant factor was the consultant's relationship with the software supplier, SAP. The better his or her contacts, the faster problems could be solved. But by no means did consultants from SAP necessarily have any better contacts than people from partner consulting companies.

Consulting company

When scouring the market for a suitable consultant we were not particularly seeking an exclusive arrangement with any one consulting company. We simply wanted the best person for the job, from whichever company. Here too we learned some useful lessons. First of all, it was not easy to find the best consultants and sign them up. Second, we found that top consultants did not necessarily fulfill our requirements: not only were we demanding a high level of expertise but also an ability to appreciate our problems and the capacity to transfer knowledge to our employees.

In the end we came to appreciate a close relationship with a single consulting company for the following reasons:

- Closer contacts provide more opportunities to build up a relationship of trust between customer and the consulting company.

- The consulting company becomes familiar with the customer's needs and preferences, and so can give better advice.
- The consulting company acquires a direct stake in the project, and so feels responsible for ensuring its success.
- It is faster and therefore more efficient to work with one consulting company.
- The customer receives fast and effective support when there are problems.
- The customer gets to hear all the latest news and tips from the SAP organization.

In our experience, most of the consultants from the better companies were of good quality. That does not mean that the others did not have good consultants; in fact all of the companies had some good people to offer, but unfortunately very few of them understood their customers' real needs.

It is amazing how many companies have not yet understood the principle of customer care. They are not responsive to customer needs, but rather have their own ideas of good practice, which relate more to their own consultants' experience and the particular implementation strategy. It should not be difficult to select consultants on the basis of the require-ments, experience, and corporate culture of the customers themselves. However, this requires a close mutual understanding between customer and consulting company.

In the end we dealt with one consulting company in Switzerland (SLI consulting) and one in the Netherlands (C/tac). These companies managed to respond very well to our needs. They sent us the right people: those who could advise us according to our needs. We continued to work on a basis of trust with those companies after implementation.

OSS, SAP's own customer hot-line, also proved an invaluable backup. Response times were not always ideal, but using the service was still a significant help in solving serious problems.

Consultancy pricing

We were amazed at the pricing variations. Daily fees ranged from SFr1,200 to SFr2,800, with ABAP programming mostly at the SFr1,200 end. Some consulting companies even charged for traveling time. Neither did paying the highest prices secure the most competent consultants.

In our experience, the following represented an acceptable arrangement:

- SFr1,800–2,200 a day for module consulting
- SFr1,600 for ABAP programming
- traveling expenses excluded
- 8 hours' working time
- traveling time to the debit of the consulting company.

The fees differ, of course, in every country. In the Netherlands, for example, the fees were comparable with those in Switzerland when converted into guilders; that would be 1,800 guilders for module consulting and 1,600 guilders for ABAP programming.

In spite of wide price variations, the consulting fee was never the main priority in employing a consultant. Trust, competence, and personality were always much more important than the fee.

Internal consulting

For the roll-out in the Welsh plant, we used an interesting alternative to external consulting. In most projects our own experienced project members acted as consultants. Following our step-by-step philosophy, these people had already implemented the same projects either in the sales area or in the Dutch plant. They possessed the unique combination of company-specific knowledge of processes and procedures together with SAP customizing experience. They knew our special customizing requirements better than any external consultant.

Advantages of internal consulting:

- **Time saving** We reduced the throughput time of our biggest projects in the Welsh plant by 50%. This put us in a comfortable position to introduce the projects seven months earlier than planned.
- **Cost savings** We saved all our consulting costs, which in our case were 23% of the running cost (see 'Running costs' in Section 4.3.3). In addition, seven months' internal and external costs were saved by the early introduction of projects. Based on our calculation of SFr80,000 for the weekly internal and external cost of any delay of the whole program, we saved the company about SFr560,000.
- **Know-how** Our people, of course, were the best acquainted with company processes procedures and organization, and were particularly well qualified when they had already implemented the project once before.
- **Customizing** The customizing went quite fast because most settings could be copied.
- **Communication** Mutual understanding increased substantially between both plants, but most notably between those departments working together.
- **Same philosophy** By using the same customizing and the same structure we were following a common philosophy in both plants.

Disadvantages of internal consulting:

- **Ownership** Project members from the second plant acquired no sense of ownership of the project as they knew they could always fall back on their colleagues at the first plant.

- **Know-how**   The system knowledge would not be so profound as at the other plant, since most settings had already been established and the major issues discussed and settled.
- **Human resources capacity**   Where the project member's role is as consultant, a resource gap could develop in both the project and the line.

4.3.3   Cost

This chapter describes our budgeting setup. It explains how we defined investment costs and running costs, and offers an overview of our budget. (For a detailed analysis of the total project costs see Section 11.2.3.)

Budgeting external costs

Recording project costs in detail is instrumental in measuring performance.

All project costs and hours were reported by our project members on a weekly basis. The project administration summarized the costs in a budget versus actual comparison, and provided the figures monthly to the steering committee.

We divided the budget into investment costs and running costs (see Table 4.4), defining investment costs as those that should be written off over several years. In our project this was related to hardware and software costs. Running costs were identified as annually recurring costs: costs that should be written off within the same year, together with depreciation costs of hardware and software.

We decided that meeting deadlines was more important than the issue of cost. We calculated the total internal and external program costs for a weekly delay at approximately SFr80,000. On completion of a project costs are forgotten, whereas missed deadlines are not. It is advisable to budget in a contingency reserve to cover unforeseen events that are likely to occur during any complex project implementation such as an ERP software package.

Investment costs

According to Table 4.5, our total investment costs of SFr1.2 million included hardware and software expenditures for the project. We spent about 50% (SFr585,000) for the complete SAP package. A further 50% (SFr600,000) was spent on hardware.

A contingency reserve is advisable for the following reasons:

- It is difficult to calculate the additional amount of hardware space needed for every module going into production.
- Every major release change is likely to use more memory, disk space, or processor speed.
- Other backup facilities may be needed to save the additional disk space required.

Table 4.4 Budget for the third year (SFr)

	HQ and Sales	Plant NL	Plant UK	Total
Investment cost				
1 Hardware				200,000
Computer extension/disk	180,000			
Miscellaneous	20,000			
Total investment cost	200,000			200,000
Running cost				
2 Consulting				535,000
SD	10,000	5,000		
FI/CO	20,000	50,000	90,000	
AM		20,000		
MM-IM/WM		5,000		
PUR		10,000		
PP		25,000	140,000	
PM		50,000	40,000	
Several	50,000	10,000	10,000	
3 Training/courses				91,000
BC	5,000	10,000	10,000	
SD	5,000			
FI/CO	5,000	10,000	10,000	
MM-IM/WM		2,000		
PP	3,000	5,000	10,000	
PM		5,000		
Several	4,000	2,000	5,000	
4 Traveling and others	120,000	50,000	60,000	230,000
5 Unisource WAN	400,000			400,000
6 Maintenance SAP	97,000			97,000
7 Maintenance HP	24,000			24,000
8 Depreciation SW/HW	240,000			240,000
Total running cost	983,000	259,000	375,000	1,617,000

You will find further information about our hardware equipment in Section 4.7.

Running costs

The total project running cost of SFr3 million included consulting (23%) and training (4%) for the different modules, traveling and accommodation (15%), wide area network from Unisource (30%), software maintenance SAP (7%), hardware maintenance HP (1.4%), and depreciation of hardware and software (21%).

- **Consulting** It is advisable to set up a project budget with enough reserves for consulting costs, because you are never sure at the beginning of a project how much consulting is required to implement an application. The standard software is not always capable of solving all the company requirements. Special programming solutions (see Section 10.5) require special and expensive consulting efforts.

Table 4.5 Total project costs (SFr '000)

	Year 1 Budget	Year 1 Actual	Year 2 Budget	Year 2 Actual	Year 3 Budget	Year 3 Actual	Total Budget	Total Actual
Investment cost								
Software SAP	600	352	240	232	0	0	840	584
Hardware	111	298	50	48	200	250	361	596
Total investment cost	711	650	290	280	200	250	1,201	1,180
Running cost								
Consulting	680	112	360	361	535	230	1,575	703
External training	105	65	74	29	91	25	270	119
Traveling and others	195	171	227	155	230	125	652	451
Unisource/Communication	364	170	360	360	400	380	1,124	910
Maintenance SAP	143	9	90	96	97	106	330	211
Maintenance HP	12	0	12	23	24	20	48	43
Depreciation HW/SW	143	143	258	258	240	240	641	641
Total running cost	1,642	670	1,381	1,282	1,617	1,126	4,640	3,078
Internal personnel cost								
Personnel (man days)	4,200	2,406	3,215	2,829	3,000	1,664	10,415	6,899
Internal personnel cost	1,260	722	965	849	900	499	3,125	2,070

- **Training** Every year we overestimated the training costs. External training should be kept to the absolute minimum; that way, people can experiment and acquire direct experience. Training is more useful in the start-up phase of the module. Customer-specific in-house training by consulting companies is cheaper and more efficient than the standard SAP courses.
- **Traveling and accommodation** As we are an international company, project activities require a lot of traveling. Therefore it is an important part of our budget.
- **Wide area network, software and hardware maintenance** These running costs not only arise during the project; they will form part of the ongoing maintenance costs of the system.

We budgeted running project costs of SFr5 million and investment costs of SFr1.2 million. With the investment costs we were on budget, and with the running costs we stayed about SFr2 million below budget. Savings targets were met in all areas, and especially in consulting. These savings arose from the faster than scheduled implementation, and thanks to our quite experienced project members, who needed less consulting and were even able to use their know-how for internal consulting of the same projects in other plants.

Internal costs

We considered only external costs in our budget. Internal costs were not budgeted. To get an idea of internal costs, we registered all hours spent on the project. This totaled some 6,900 man-days. Estimating a daily total salary cost of about SFr300, the project would need an additional SFr2.1 million.

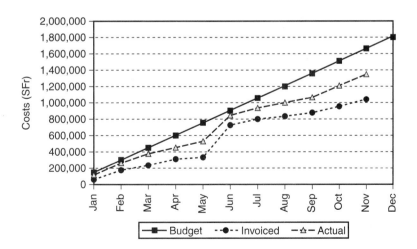

Figure 4.3 Budgeted cost graph of 3rd year.

Estimating budgeted cost

According to the steering committee requirements, we visualized costs as shown in Figure 4.3. The graphs show the following information:

1. Budgeted costs.
2. Actual costs, including received but not yet invoiced services.
3. Invoiced costs, which correspond with invoices actually received.

4.3.4   Lessons learned for project resources

1. **Build up trust among the project members**   Trust among the project members, including the steering committee, is essential for a successful project, because the project organization has hardly any hierarchical authority but has to be based on natural authority, that is, trust. Unless trust is established, the project will require intensive supervision and coaching in order to prevent rapid decline. Trust can be generated through effective communication, coaching, delegation of responsibility, personal support, etc.

2. **Establish management ownership**   The top management must play an active role on the steering committee, and assume owner-ship. Having ownership means feeling responsible for the project, supporting it, and providing it with the appropriate authority and resources. Endorsement by top managers enforces the project acceptance throughout the company.

   Departmental managers must be members of the project team to adapt ownership, contribute the necessary line know-how, and avoid losing touch.

   The assumption of ownership by the department manager is once again a clear signal to departmental staff to accept the project. Furthermore, the departmental manager is usually the best acquainted with the processes and procedures of that depart-ment, and so is the best qualified to support the project in it. Participation is also the best insurance against losing touch with the newly designed processes and procedures, and the best way of exploiting the system's full potential in the future.

3. **Appoint a strong and effective management team**   The project management has to lead, manage, and coach the whole project: the stronger it is, the better the chances for a successful project implementation. If the project management is below par in its tasks and responsibilities, the project is likely to fail because project management is the key role in the whole project.

4. **Empower project management sufficiently**   The project man-agement must have wide-ranging authority and control over all

aspects of the project. Project management must be able to act independently, quickly, and effectively, regardless of any potential obstacles within the organization.

5. **Appoint a well-qualified and versatile project management team** The team should be highly competent in all aspects of the project so as to be able to react rapidly and effectively to project problems. Their authority should be such as to enable them to take all the necessary managerial and technical measures across any organizational barriers.

6. **Recruit capable project members** Project work is very demanding and complex, and therefore requires people with a high learning potential. This is crucial for project managers, who, as the driving force of the entire project, must be of particularly high calibre. Likewise, project members from the line organization must be skilled individuals, capable of delivering a fast and effective implementation. The project organization is only as good as the individuals in it.

7. **Define tasks and responsibilities clearly** Clearly defined tasks and responsibilities at all levels of the project organization contribute to the efficiency of the project, and help to reduce conflicts of authority and jurisdiction. Every project member, including the external consultant, must understand exactly the project goals and strategy as well as their own tasks and responsibilities within it.

8. **Engage full-time project members** A project has to be staffed with sufficient human resources. The key members in particular must be available full-time to guarantee continuity and progress. If this is not the case, the project is likely to lose momentum, and ultimately will degenerate. Part-time project members always tend to work for the line organization because line matters have higher priority to them and are less complex than project work.

9. **Ensure that the capabilities and skills of the project members match the project job requirements** If any project members are not suited to the work, the project will suffer, more or less, according to the strategic importance of their role. To compensate for any such weakness, special support would be required from other project members, not least from the project leader or manager.

10. **Include line experience in the project team** This should be provided by experienced people from the department where the module will be implemented. The line manager and another skilled departmental employee represent an ideal combination.

11. **Learn from qualified external consultants** The complex implementation of an ERP software package calls for a high degree of skill and competence. The success of a project depends heavily

on the capabilities of the consultants with intimate knowledge of the software. Hence good consultants have a major impact on the throughput time and the quality of a project. An external consultant at the project team level has to help with customizing, setting up the implementation schedule, and supervising the project. A consultant at the steering committee level has to advise the project concerning organization, processes, and procedures, and support the project manager in his role.

12. **Establish a relationship of trust with a consulting company** Where there is a close relationship, and the consulting company understands the customer's preferences and needs, the quality of consulting is better. The consulting company assumes a stake in the project's success, and where problems arise the customer receives faster support as well as being kept up to date in SAP.

13. **Avoid budget shortfalls** It is advisable to set up a project budget with enough reserves to cover unforeseeable costs. The external consulting input is especially difficult to quantify, as it depends strongly on the capabilities of the project members. A budget shortfall may delay the project considerably, as financial resources are not easy to obtain during a project period.

14. **Keep the throughput time as short as possible** Every project is an additional load for the line organization and the members working in the project. With a short throughput time, cost is kept low, and the motivation of the project members high.

4.4   Project administration

Project administration includes: all matters relating to progress reporting; time registration; the organization of meetings; the distribution of project information; the arrangement of project facilities; the outlining of project standards; and the writing of a project handbook.

4.4.1   Reporting

We differentiate between weekly and progress reporting. Weekly reporting covers all activities carried out during the past week and planned for the following week. Progress reporting measures progress against time.

Weekly reporting

Purpose of weekly reporting

Weekly reporting is a very important tool for all project members, and serves the following functions:

- **Progress control** For the project manager and the project leader it is a tool for monitoring progress closely. They should study the weekly reporting carefully (see Appendix, Figure A.2 and Appendix, Figure A.3) to detect any bottlenecks. Based on the reported information, corrective actions may be needed.
- **Risk identification** The outstanding issues mentioned on the report form are a good indication of potential risk for the project. Risks need to be investigated and discussed within the project organization, starting bottom up, until a solution is found.
- **Organization** The project members often find weekly reporting annoying and unnecessary. In fact it is an invaluable organizational aid. Itemizing all the activities done over the past week can reinforce the sense of achievement. Planning the next week's work helps them to anticipate potential problems or bottlenecks.
- **Project information** Weekly reporting provides progress information to all project members, and indicates whether the project is on schedule or not. The information is especially valuable for the steering committee to get an idea of progress.
- **Feedback on working time** The reports also show the time spent on the project. This is a good indicator of the project members' workload. If actual time spent is more or if it less than scheduled, the appropriate measures should be taken (see Section 8.2.4).

Weekly reporting procedure

The project team members report to their project leader using the standard report form (see Appendix, Figure A.3). The project members record:

- time spent by project member
- expenses of project member
- activities performed in the reporting week
- activities next week
- outstanding issues.

The project leader reports directly to the project manager using the standard form (see Appendix, Figure A.2). In addition to the project members' information, the project leader comments on the overall project status, estimating whether or not it is running on schedule.

With this information the project manager now:

- Investigates the outstanding issues.
- Aggregates time spent and costs, recording them against the budget (see Table 4.6).
- Considers whether the time spent is sufficient.
- Takes a close look at the activities done last week and those planned for the coming week, and compares them with the project implementation schedule.

Table 4.6 Time recording sheet

Module	Project member	Budget in %/month	Actual in %/month	Budget in hours/month	Actual in hours/month	Week 40	Week 41	Week 42	Week 43	Week 44	Week 45	Week 46	Week 47	Week 48
FI SKL	HD	100	52	152.0	79	36	11	10	22	20				
	HR	40	13	60.8	19	10	4	0	5	4				
	MEP	20	3	32.0	4	0	4	0	0	8				
PM SKL	BS	10	18	15.2	28	7	8	5	8	8				
	RBR	80	68	122.0	103	30	28	19	26	24				
FI SUK	ADP	60	40	90.0	60	24	14	6	16	30				
	AOK	60	33	90.0	50	24	10	8	8	24				
PP SUK	KGW	100	97	150.0	145	37	41	36	31	40				
	ALG	40	13	60.0	20	2	13	3	2	2				
	IW	40	7	60.0	11	2	6	2	1	0				
	SWL	20	13	30.0	19	2	7	7	3	2				
	GBS	20	29	30.0	44		16	20	8	22				
	XB	20	12	30.0	18		16	2	0	16				
PM SUK	RTT	80	59	120.0	88	23	23	23	19	23				
PUR SUK	SW	40	5	60.0	7	4	2	0	1	1				
	SRT	20	5	30.0	7	4	2	0	1	1				
IT	DH	50	20	80.0	32	10	12	10	0	12				
	EL	80	49	128.0	79	26	24	20	9	11				
	AFJ	80	55	120.0	83	16	25	27	15	15				
	DAZ	40	72	60.0	108	31	30	29	19	31				
TOTAL	Total			2759.0	1286									

HQ CH: 40 hours/week   160
Plant NL: 38 hours/week   152
Plant UK: 37.5 hours/week   150

Working hours per country (1 year = 1600 hours):

Sales office FR: 39 hours/week   156
Sales office UK: 35 hours/week   140
Sales office IT: 40 hours/week   160

Sales office ES: 41 hours/week   164
Sales office NL: 40 hours/week   160
Sales office DE: 38 hours/week   152

- Controls the progress of the projects.
- Sends the project summary (Appendix, Figure A.4) to the project leaders and the steering committee members.

Frequency of reporting

We opted for weekly reporting, since daily reporting created excessive administration, and fortnightly reporting meant that people would have forgotten the previous fortnight's activities. The reports had to be sent every Friday by 1200 (CET) at the latest by e-mail to the project secretary.

Every Friday we faced the same problem: we had to remind the project leaders to hand in their reports. Our project secretary usually prepared some nasty reminders in advance, and sent them out by e-mail after 1200 CET. In the last resort, the secretary would call the project leaders to account for the delay, and listened to their interesting excuses. Finally the secretary managed to get the reports.

Progress reporting

Progress was tracked over a certain period of time, usually the time between two meetings. We used the report form (see Appendix, Figure A.6) to ensure standardized reporting from the project management team and the steering committee meetings.

The progress report form registers the following information:

- The header indicates the module specification, project location, type, and date of meeting.
- The milestones overview shows the progress per milestone as a percentage. The milestones are based on the four phases mentioned in the implementation schedule: planning, realization, preparation, and productive phase.
- The current status describes all activities since the last meeting.
- Future activities include important tasks to be tackled before the next meeting.
- 'Outstanding issues' refers to project problems that are relevant, and which should be discussed in the meeting.

This standardized progress report form helped all meeting members to see at a glance progress, activities, and problems of a project.

4.4.2 Time recording

Each project member was allocated an agreed number of hours as a percentage (see Section 4.3.1 under 'Human resources participation'). From the normal working hours at the site where the project member was employed, we calculated the weekly, monthly, and yearly working hours for the project budget. Based on the weekly report we recorded the hours in the time registration sheet shown in Table 4.6. This time sheet is the basis for the human resources control shown in Figure 8.3.

If people did not put in the agreed hours we inquired into the reason. In some cases we simply adjusted the agreed time to the real need of that individual, adjusting the agreed percentage to the actual. Measures to be taken to improve the project member participation are described in 'Provision of human resources' in Section 4.3.1.

4.4.3   Meeting management techniques

Meetings as a fundamental part of project work

Meetings are an essential part of the project work, and are certainly not a waste of time. They are justified on the following grounds:

- **Communication** With every meeting the project members improve their communication and mutual understanding.
- **Progress control** Regular meetings help to monitor progress and provide feedback on all issues.
- **Throughput time** Efficient and effective meetings have a considerable impact on the project throughput time, because decision-making is better, and problem-solving is faster.
- **Teamwork** In meetings the project members start to understand each other better, learn to accept and respect individual strengths and weaknesses, and resolve conflicts and problems that have already been raised and discussed.
- **Project quality** Frequent meetings improve quality because the project members form a team, and a more pleasant atmosphere evolves. Discussions are more focused, and hence better decisions are taken.

The frequency of the meetings has a direct impact on the throughput time: the more often meetings are held, the more efficient and effective they are.

Meeting agenda

Good meetings are well prepared in advance: the better the preparation is, the more efficient and satisfying for the participants. The first preparatory step for a meeting is to set up the agenda. Consider the type of information required by the participants. To ensure the inclusion of all items it is helpful to keep an open file between meetings.

The agenda for a meeting may consist of the items mentioned below. (A typical example of an agenda for a project management team meeting can be found in the Appendix, Figure A.5.)

1. Timing
2. Project organization
3. Progress reporting
4. Time and costs
5. Special issues
6. Miscellaneous
7. Date of next meeting

Below you will find a short explanation of the above-mentioned agenda points:

- **Timing** Strict time limits should be set for the discussion of each agenda item. The time allocation is decided before the meeting and closely monitored during it, otherwise you will always run out of time.
- **Project organization** Minutes of the last meeting are approved and any changes in project organization or planning announced.
- **Progress reporting** Each project member reports on progress, status, activities, and problems since last meeting (see Section 4.4.1).
- **Time and costs** Recorded working time (see Figure 8.3) and expenditure are discussed (see Figure 4.3).
- **Special issues** Here the members raise and intensively discuss all matters such as the as-is and to-be concepts or the critical issues which have arisen over the month and which seriously threaten the project unless resolved.
- **Miscellaneous** Announcements are made about project matters not requiring any extensive debate or discussion.

It is important to provide as much information as possible before the meeting. People must have time for a serious preparation. An explanation of the different agenda items helps the participants to understand what they are expected to prepare. The explanation can be provided in a separate document. Another idea is just to write below every agenda item the questions to be answered during the meeting. An excellent way is also to sit together with the participants to prepare the meeting. But this, of course, is not always possible and does not eliminate the need for the explanatory document since all the relevant issues are not always identified at the preparatory talks.

The agenda should be sent at least a week in advance to the participants in order to give them a chance to react, ask questions or add items to the agenda. If the agenda is changed, a revised agenda must be forwarded to the participants. If there is no time for this, participants should be notified of the changes at the start of the meeting and a copy of the new agenda distributed.

Tips for the preparation of a meeting

Based on our experience, we made a rough guide for the meeting's chairman as an aid to better preparation:

- Meetings should be held only when necessary, otherwise the participants' attention will wander, and the meeting will lose momentum.
- Short but frequent meetings are more efficient than long but less regular ones.
- Good preparation improves the quality of a meeting tremendously.
- People tend to prepare poorly for meetings. Encourage better preparation by stating speakers' names on the agenda. This will also strengthen their sense of ownership.
- A copy of the steering committee agenda should be sent to the project management team members, since they must help prepare the steering committee meeting.
- The chairman's name should feature as little as possible on the agenda, since the chairman needs to lead the meeting.
- The goal of a meeting is to reach conclusions and decisions and not to get lost in endless discussions. To pre-empt this, every participant should be well-briefed in advance, and thorny problems should be raised and discussed beforehand.
- Topics that could be dealt with bilaterally should not be put on the meeting agenda.
- The project manager should brief the steering committee chairman before the meeting on the decisions he wants to push through.
- Slides should be produced in a readable font size and not be too dense, summarizing only the main points.
- Schedule or expenditure graphs should indicate deviations with an arrow or special color to highlight the issues. Digressions will bore the listeners and waste precious meeting time.
- Specific issues should be presented by the appropriate specialists. In case they are not an official member of the meeting, they have to be invited for the particular presentation.
- Guest presentations should be checked beforehand to ensure that they are appropriate.
- The meeting room has to be checked and arranged well in advance. It is advisable to be there before the meeting starts, to avoid any surprises.

Essential etiquette for meetings

The following tips apply not only to the chairman but to all the participants of a meeting:

- The atmosphere is crucial in a meeting. Conducting meetings in a pleasant atmosphere is more productive, and leads to better decisions being taken.

- Seek consensus on controversial decisions, and avoid leaving unresolved issues or contention between participants.
- It is never good to take people by surprise with totally new proposals, since they have had no time to absorb the implications and may become tense as a result.
- Sometimes it pays to ask for wisdom rather than convince with good arguments.
- Don't become emotional. Over-heated arguments are always counter-productive because objectivity is lost.
- Take care that you don't get too tense defending a topic. Sometimes a smile is more convincing than any amount of rational argument. Tension undermines confidence.
- Give the impression of a smiling, relaxed, and unstressed meeting chairman. A relaxed, smiling chairman can calm things down.
- Try to neutralize people's natural aggression when defending 'their territory' before other participants.
- The quality of a meeting depends on the contribution of the participants: the better they are prepared, the better the meeting.
- 'Hit and run': once an idea has been accepted it is unwise to continue justifying it since this would be to invite further objections and risk opening the issue once again; this time you may lose the argument.
- When you get things completely your own way you are well advised not to labour the point. Try to hide it and continue with the next agenda point.
- When guest speakers are present they should be allowed to participate in non-controversial decisions arising from their particular contribution.
- Presentations are best limited to key aspects, particularly threats. Key information should be clearly distinguished from interesting observations so as not to over-complicate things and drag the meeting out.
- It is useful to conclude with a short debriefing, to get some feedback on your performance and assess reactions.

Personal contact outside meetings is still very important. Often problems are not mentioned in an official meeting because they are too embarrassing for the person involved. Furthermore you will get the best insight into the project by talking to the project members personally.

Minutes

Here are a few hints:

- A secretary should take the minutes so that participants can fully concentrate on the meeting and yet all the important information has been included.
- An open issue list has to be set at the beginning of the minutes, as this is the most important part of them.

- Never make anybody responsible for an open issue without setting a deadline, otherwise supervision becomes difficult.
- Send confidential topics by separate mail.

See an example of the minutes in the Appendix, Figure A.7.

Project team meetings

The project leaders are obliged to hold periodic meetings. A copy of the minutes should be sent to the project manager to keep him informed about the progress. A standard template for the minutes is helpful to the project teams.

4.4.4   Information and communication

Good information is a critical success factor in project implementation. Open and honest information and communication is of paramount importance to satisfy the users' information requirements and to prevent rumors. The users need this information because any project brings changes to their working environment, and is basically something that threatens their job. The open information and communication policy helps the user to become acquainted with the new situation, builds up trust in the project and among its members, and promotes acceptance of the project.

Project marketing

It is primarily the project manager's task to market the project and to keep the company informed about the project activities. The project members must also play their part in selling the project by helping to convince people of its benefits.

The following marketing opportunities should be taken:

- Publishing of a project bulletin (see 'Project bulletin' below).
- Publishing articles in company magazines or newspapers.
- Making project presentations in other, not directly project-related meetings (sales, plant, year-end meetings, etc.).
- Standard presentation training for project leaders.
- Personal chats with interested parties, line managers, and users.
- Special publicity for the live date of a module.
- Availability of all project information to the whole company on the intranet.

Project bulletin

An excellent tool to update the company on project activities is the publishing of a monthly bulletin (see Appendix, Figure A.8).

The effort required to produce this monthly bulletin (about two days a month) is insignificant compared with its positive impact. Below are a few tips on how to keep the workload down, and make the bulletin interesting to read:

- The bulletin can be structured as follows: cover article of a project member, photograph and profile of the author, project news.
- Visually attractive pictures and graphs improve readability.
- Project members and users themselves should write the articles rather than the project administration. Project members and users are more in touch with the readers, and the project administration need only coordinate, edit, and publish the bulletin.
- In the first issue of the bulletin and during difficult phases of the project, articles and photographs of decision-makers should be published so people realize that the project is fully backed by the top management.
- People appreciate open and honest communication, and so even negative project news should be reported. Readers are skeptical about endlessly positive reports, and the credibility of the bulletin will suffer.
- Most people, regardless of age or position, are flattered by appearing in print. It is important, however, that the project manager stays in the background.

A bulletin brings various benefits for the company:

- The company is constantly updated on the project progress.
- As people are familiarized with the project they lose their initial fear of it.
- Not only project members but also other employees can learn from the experience gained from it.
- The company is well-prepared for the implementation.
- The bulletin contributes to mutual understanding by giving an insight into the organization, processes, and procedures of other departments, and by showing people's different lifestyles.

Significantly, users respond well to being entrusted with some negative information; it is taken as a sign of confidence and respect.

4.4.5   Project facilities

The project team must have an optimal working environment, with appropriate software and hardware; flipcharts; an overhead projector; a library; access to project information, etc. This does not necessarily mean relocating people's offices to the project room, but at least they must be able to meet there and engage in project work. The room itself should be comfortable and conducive to meetings.

A good project room promotes:

- efficiency
- creativity
- project spirit
- communication.

4.4.6　Project standards

Purpose of standards

The definition of standards in a project brings the following advantages:

- **Compatibility**　Everybody is able to read or link the documents and files from other projects (e.g. for a common documentation of the projects).
- **Efficiency**　Having all the standard documents to hand facilitates the project members' work (reporting, writing minutes and agendas, implementation schedule, etc.).
- **Transparency**　The origin or the author of a document, file, or program can be easily identified.

Definition of standards

We found it useful to define standards in the following areas:

- Hardware and software (standards according to our IT policy).
- Papers and documents (see Appendix for examples on documents).
- File formats and file names.
- Meeting agenda and minutes, reporting, implementation schedule.
- Programming guidelines (see 'Programming guidelines' in Section 4.7.2).

4.4.7　Project handbook

The project handbook includes the written statement about project scope, project organization, project resources, planning of activities, project administration, project control, and risk management. It is a guide for all future activities in the project, and a reference for everybody involved in it. It helps the team to get prepared and started.

The project handbook should contain the information listed in Table 4.7. All items are detailed in later chapters.

4.4.8　Lessons learned for project administration

1. **Organize periodic reporting**　Periodic reporting is a way to track progress; to identify potential or real problems; to update project members on progress; and to help them plan their weekly activities. Project management also get feedback from the reporting on time spent and workload of project members.

Table 4.7 Contents of project handbook

1.   Project scope (see Section 4.1)
     1.1   Project definition
     1.2   Project objectives
     1.3   Project strategy
2.   Project organization (see Section 4.2)
3.   Project resources (see Section 4.3)
     3.1   Human resources
     3.2   Cost
4.   Project implementation plan (see Section 4.5)
5.   Project administration (see Section 4.4)
     5.1   Reporting
     5.2   Time recording
     5.3   Meeting management techniques
     5.4   Communication and information
     5.5   Project facilities
     5.6   Project standards
6.   Project control (Section 8.2) and risk management (Section 8.3)

2.   **Hold regular meetings**   Regular meetings are an important part of project work. They improve communication, monitor progress closely, and encourage teamwork. These factors contribute considerably to project quality and throughput time, because the quality of decisions is enhanced, and problems are solved faster.

3.   **Choose a high frequency for meetings**   The frequency of the meetings has a direct impact on the throughput time: the more often meetings are held, the more efficient and effective they are.

4.   **Prepare meetings thoroughly**   The result is a more efficient and effective meeting. It is essential to provide the necessary information before the meeting to ensure a good preparation of the participants. Preparatory work includes gathering information and even discussing potentially difficult topics before the meeting.

5.   **Enforce good etiquette in meetings**   The chairman must keep everyone's emotions in check and promote an atmosphere conducive to rational and objective discussion. Consensus should be sought on controversial issues so as to prevent any lingering bad feelings or unresolved contention among participants. Sometimes it is better to ask for wisdom instead of always insisting on unanimity.

6.   **Communicate openly and frankly**   This is indispensable so as to inform the users adequately and to discourage rumors. After all, any project that brings changes to the working environment is potentially threatening to their jobs. With an open information policy, the users can familiarize themselves with the new situation, and learn to trust and finally accept the project and its representatives.

7. **Sell the project** The project has to be sold within the company to improve understanding and acceptance. Various marketing activities have to be planned to promote the project idea. Every project member should help to sell.
8. **Create a project handbook** The project handbook summarizes the most important matters of the project. It is a guide for all future activities in the project, and a reference for everybody involved in the project. It helps the project team to get organized and started.

4.5 Project implementation plan

We planned all our activities in an implementation schedule. These are organized according to the project life cycle as in Section 2.1. The schedule represents a complete overview of the project implementation. The following sections describe how it is created and the software tool is used.

The implementation schedule is of course the most important tool for measuring progress, and is discussed in Section 8.2.3.

4.5.1 Creation of an implementation schedule

The implementation schedule has to be created in collaboration with the project team, the consultant, and the project manager. The project team brings in its expert know-how from the line side, the consultant his knowledge of the software, and the project manager his skills in general and project management.

To estimate the duration of a specific task in an implementation schedule demands an intimate knowledge of the software, which the team does not usually have at the beginning. This is where an experienced consultant is needed. If the consultant is a member of the project team, he or she has to be made responsible for the creation of the implementation schedule.

The whole planning of the implementation schedule is a democratic process. The team should collaborate with the project manager to set targets. The project manager checks and approves the implementation schedule. In doing this, he or she must take all the modules into account, and make sure the implementation schedule is tight but realistic. If the timescale is too short, the deadline will likely be missed; if too long, the project will lose its momentum.

Once all the activities and targets are set, the team can be assessed against their own schedule and milestones. After all, the project team is measured on their own setup time schedule and targets.

Planning is an ongoing process. Therefore project activities and resources must be organized on the basis of the information to hand at the start of the project. Of course, as more knowledge is acquired, the planning can be adjusted, but keeping the original milestones. The schedule must cover all relevant tasks, since if any are omitted it could seriously undermine the project.

In our first projects we overlooked the various public holidays and project member holidays. This endangered the project deadline, and could be compensated only with additional work and postponement of certain holidays.

The full implementation schedule lists all project activities and tasks exhaustively. Figure 4.4 outlines the main tasks. The time recorded is an average of days. A detailed implementation schedule listing all tasks is shown in the Appendix, Figure A.9.

The following information may be included under 'tasks':

- Task name: definition of the task.
- Completed: a percentage figure from 0 to 100%, depending on how many tasks per item are completed.
- Duration: amount of throughput time used to complete the task.
- Start and finish: planned starting and finishing date of the task.
- Actual finish: actual finishing date of the task.
- Resources: human resources used for the specific task.

The milestones in an implementation schedule usually represent the end of a project phase. As all the goals for a project phase are linked to the milestones, they give good feedback on the progress of the project.

To estimate the duration of a particular task demands an in-depth knowledge of the module, which the project team does not usually have at the beginning. This is where an experienced consultant is needed. If that consultant is a member of the project team, they should be made responsible for the creation of the implementation schedule.

4.5.2 Project management software

The use of a project management package (such as Microsoft Project) is highly recommended, because these programs offer features for recording the activities in a project. We used the package mainly for the following:

- creating an implementation schedule
- creating links to other tasks
- assigning costs and human resources
- using Gantt charts to track progress
- attaching notes.

Of course, a software package offers many more features than just the above. We tried to keep things as simple as possible, since excessive bureaucracy can stifle creativity.

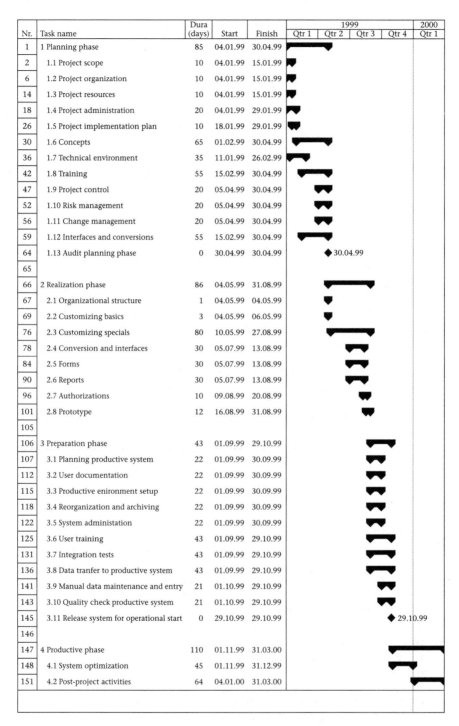

Nr.	Task name	Dura (days)	Start	Finish	1999 Qtr 1	Qtr 2	Qtr 3	Qtr 4	2000 Qtr 1
1	1 Planning phase	85	04.01.99	30.04.99					
2	1.1 Project scope	10	04.01.99	15.01.99					
6	1.2 Project organization	10	04.01.99	15.01.99					
14	1.3 Project resources	10	04.01.99	15.01.99					
18	1.4 Project administration	20	04.01.99	29.01.99					
26	1.5 Project implementation plan	10	18.01.99	29.01.99					
30	1.6 Concepts	65	01.02.99	30.04.99					
36	1.7 Technical environment	35	11.01.99	26.02.99					
42	1.8 Training	55	15.02.99	30.04.99					
47	1.9 Project control	20	05.04.99	30.04.99					
52	1.10 Risk management	20	05.04.99	30.04.99					
56	1.11 Change management	20	05.04.99	30.04.99					
59	1.12 Interfaces and conversions	55	15.02.99	30.04.99					
64	1.13 Audit planning phase	0	30.04.99	30.04.99		◆ 30.04.99			
65									
66	2 Realization phase	86	04.05.99	31.08.99					
67	2.1 Organizational structure	1	04.05.99	04.05.99					
69	2.2 Customizing basics	3	04.05.99	06.05.99					
76	2.3 Customizing specials	80	10.05.99	27.08.99					
78	2.4 Conversion and interfaces	30	05.07.99	13.08.99					
84	2.5 Forms	30	05.07.99	13.08.99					
90	2.6 Reports	30	05.07.99	13.08.99					
96	2.7 Authorizations	10	09.08.99	20.08.99					
101	2.8 Prototype	12	16.08.99	31.08.99					
105									
106	3 Preparation phase	43	01.09.99	29.10.99					
107	3.1 Planning productive system	22	01.09.99	30.09.99					
112	3.2 User documentation	22	01.09.99	30.09.99					
115	3.3 Productive enironment setup	22	01.09.99	30.09.99					
118	3.4 Reorganization and archiving	22	01.09.99	30.09.99					
122	3.5 System administation	22	01.09.99	30.09.99					
125	3.6 User training	43	01.09.99	29.10.99					
131	3.7 Integration tests	43	01.09.99	29.10.99					
136	3.8 Data tranfer to productive system	43	01.09.99	29.10.99					
141	3.9 Manual data maintenance and entry	21	01.10.99	29.10.99					
143	3.10 Quality check productive system	21	01.10.99	29.10.99					
145	3.11 Release system for operational start	0	29.10.99	29.10.99				◆ 29.10.99	
146									
147	4 Productive phase	110	01.11.99	31.03.00					
148	4.1 System optimization	45	01.11.99	31.12.99					
151	4.2 Post-project activities	64	04.01.00	31.03.00					

Figure 4.4   Generic implementation schedule (duration as example).

4.5.3 Lessons learned for project implementation plan

1. **Make sure the implementation schedule covers all necessary tasks** The implementation schedule is the progress-monitoring tool and the script for the project. Missing tasks may impact negatively on the project.

2. **Use consultants when creating the schedule** An experienced external consultant is probably the best source of module-specific knowledge necessary when estimating the duration of activities on the schedule.

3. **Plan sufficient contingency into the schedule** Flexibility is required to cover unforeseeable events that commonly occur. A shortage of time weakens and ultimately endangers the project.

4. **Plan democratically, execute directively** Setting targets is a collaborative process between the project manager and the project team. Thereafter performance can be judged against the team's own criteria.

5. **Take holidays and absences into account when planning** Holidays, whether personal, public, or religious, along with issues such as plant closure, are often overlooked in the planning process, but have potentially serious implications for deadlines.

6. **Keep the planning simple and non-bureaucratic** The planning tools must serve their purpose without being unnecessarily complex. If they are over-bureaucratic they may stifle creativity.

4.6 Concepts

The as-is concept describes the current organization, its processes, and procedures. It should highlight problems within existing structures, draw attention to procedural shortcomings, and stimulate new ideas.

The to-be concept proceeds from the as-is concept to describe the future organization, processes, and procedures of the department. The department should be very closely involved in the creation of the to-be concept because this is its own future. The to-be concept has to consider the limits prescribed by the standard software: hence the necessity of engaging a consultant with an intimate knowledge of the software and its limitations. The better the to-be concept is formulated, the faster will be the progress in the subsequent phases, because the necessary decisions concerning the future structures have been taken and agreed upon. Once this is done, the project team has clear guidelines, and can work efficiently without repetitive and contro-versial discussions with line management about project objectives and strategy.

It is important that these concepts are formulated during the planning phase because they are the foundation for the subsequent phases of the project. The concepts have to be in line with the general company strategy.

4.6.1   As-is concept

Description of content

The as-is concept describes the future status of the organization, processes, procedures and methods in the company. It is the basis for the to-be concept.

During the implementation of our various projects we drew up the table of contents for the as-is concept listed in Table 4.8.

Management summary

A management summary is included for quick and easy reference. It offers a strategic overview of the main issues and problems arising from the concepts.

General description

- **Company and department** Gives a general introduction to the company and the departments concerned; explains the business environment of the company/department, market, turnover, strategy, and policy.
- **Organizational structure**   Describes the respective role of each part of the organization.

Table 4.8 Table of contents for the as-is concept

Management summary
1. General description
    1.1   Company and department
    1.2   Organizational structure
2. Detailed description
    2.1   Master data
    2.2   Processes
    2.3   Functions and procedures
3. Special topics
    3.1   Reports
    3.2   Forms
    3.3   Interfaces
    3.4   Authorizations
4. Measurement of performance
5. Conclusions
    5.1   Key problems
    5.2   Recommendations
6. Appendices

Detailed description

- **Master data** The core static data: detailed product descriptions, including product ranges, product groups, technical aspects, product type, etc., as used in almost all modules. Comprehensive information on customers is used in the sales and distribution environment, and so on.
- **Processes, functions and procedures** Relates to each module, and includes an indication of weaknesses in the current system.

Special topics

- **Reports and forms** It is important to make a complete inventory of all reports and forms in current use. Their present and future use can then be re-evaluated by those who use them. These documents should be described, with copies included in the appendix.
- **Interfaces** All existing links to other modules or interfaces to other programs and databases have to be described and illustrated.
- **Authorization** The authorizations have to be listed and used as a discussion basis for the to-be concept, especially in the areas of purchasing and asset management.

Measurement of performance

A list of all performance measures must clearly indicate purpose, frequency, reporting method, unit of measurement, etc.

Conclusions

Here the key problems of the current setup should be identified and described. This allows the project team or line management to pinpoint gaps and come up with new ideas.

Appendix

This collection of forms and reports used for the specific module is a good basis for discussing the to-be situation. Only when all of these documents are listed in this way do people appreciate just how many there really are.

4.6.2 To-be concept

Purpose of the to-be concept

The to-be concept describes the future organization, processes, procedures, and methods within a department and/or company. It is the basis for the realization phase of a project, and therefore must be written before starting with the second phase as in Figure 2.1 (see page 5).

The to-be concept fulfills several purposes:

- **As a foundation** It underpins the whole project, and heralds the future of the department.
- **As a list of objectives** These are clearly formulated and agreed upon.
- **As a guideline** With its detailed project definition it serves as the terms of reference for both the project team and the line organization. Likewise it gives a useful overview of the project.
- **As an organizational aid** Writing a to-be concept encourages good planning. It forces the project team and the line to review organization, processes, and procedures thoroughly.
- **As an insurance** Once approved by the steering committee, the to-be concept insures against repetitive and pointless controversial discussions. It also serves to enforce ownership of the concept by all those who have approved it. A list of their signatures may be appended.
- **For project promotion** Publishing and distributing the to-be concept serves to publicize and promote the project idea throughout the company.
- **For education** A to-be concept should inform all those concerned. It should help everyone to understand and take an informed position on the changes.
- **For change management** Setting up the to-be concept is an opportunity for all involved to critically analyze and question the existing organization, processes, and procedures. It is a motivator for change.
- **As a problem detector** Looking at the project from the end backward, the to-be concept enables project members to pinpoint problems and gaps, and set about resolving them at the earliest opportunity.

Software guidelines for the to-be concept

When implementing an ERP package such as SAP, company strategy must follow the processes described in the standard software, and not the other way around. Hence it is essential to know the organization, processes, procedures, and methods of the ERP package. As not all features of the software are known at the time of writing the to-be concept, it is essential to have an experienced consultant on hand who is able to point out the software's characteristics. Additional help can be provided by a fast implementation methodology tool offered by consulting companies or SAP (ASAP Methodology). This tool helps to simulate all processes of a company, and gives you an idea of time, schedule, processes, and procedures of a project.

Yet even this does not totally eliminate the possibility of changes in the to-be concept during the implementation phase, because the software is not known in detail. The to-be concept must be worked out in such a way as to preclude major change, leaving only minor adjustments to be made where necessary.

Responsibility for the to-be concept

It is the line manager's task to create the to-be concept for his department. The project team will support and consult the line manager, especially in questions concerning the limitations of the standard software; but the line manager must invest the necessary time to create the to-be concept, because it represents the future of that department. Neglecting this, line managers would lose control over processes and procedures within their own departments, no longer understanding them. This in turn would mean that decisions necessary for the project to proceed are not taken, and the project is delayed.

Description of content

The table of contents for the to-be concept is listed in Table 4.9.

Management summary

The management summary gives a résumé of the to-be concept. Along with a synopsis of the most important chapters it should highlight the following items in particular:

- New or changed processes, procedures, and methods compared with the as-is situation.
- Advantages/disadvantages of the new or changed processes, procedures, and methods.
- Key problems to be solved by the project team and/or by the management before and after the implementation.
- Advantages/disadvantages of the implementation.
- Concerns of the project team.

Table 4.9 Table of contents for the to-be concept

Management summary

1. Detailed description
    - 1.1   Master data
    - 1.2   Processes
    - 1.3   Functions and procedures
2. Special topics
    - 2.1   Reports
    - 2.2   Forms
    - 2.3   Interfaces
    - 2.4   Conversion
    - 2.5   Authorizations
    - 2.6   System management
3. Performance measures
4. Conclusions
    - 4.1   SWOT analysis
    - 4.2   Action list
5. Appendices

Detailed description of to-be concept

- **Master data** Defines the master data needed; describes the setup and maintenance of master data in the system; identifies the person responsible for maintenance of master data.
- **Processes** Describes the overall processes of the module, and in particular the modifications or innovations proposed by the project team.
- **Functions and procedures** Describes new or changed functions and procedures within the implementation module. The steering committee and line management must discuss and approve any changes to processes, functions, and/or procedures before they are adopted.

Special topics

- **Reports** The reporting requirements have to be noted in the to-be situation, to make everybody aware of what reports are needed and what will be available.
- **Forms** The forms are a very delicate matter for a company, and have to be discussed and illustrated in the to-be concept.
- **Interfaces** Possible interfaces and links to other modules or other programs have to be investigated, and described clearly and fully, in order to avoid later incompatibilities with other business functions.
- **Conversion** A procedure has to describe how the data conversion is planned from other programs. A calculation about the amount of data to be transferred has to be set up.
- **Authorizations** Authorizations have to be defined and discussed with the line management.
- **System management** A person should be appointed to take charge of the module after introduction.

Performance measurements

The main goal of performance measurements is to provide periodic information about the cost-effectiveness and quality-effectiveness of a process. They are necessary to improve and optimize business processes. A process should be judged not only against one performance indicator but against a whole set of different performance measurements. The frequency and sources of measurement may vary. Table 4.10 gives an example of possible logistics performance measurements.

SAP offers different standard performance measurements such as the Logistics Information System (LIS) and the Sales Information System (SIS). If the SAP model does not fit the requirements, user-specific reports have to be programmed.

Table 4.10 Example of logistics performance measurements

Type	Performance measurement	Reason	Frequency logistics	Frequency financial	Recipients	Source
Logistics	Throughput time	• Monitor standards • Input/output deviation • Lead-time deviation	Weekly/monthly	Not available	Production Logistics	Production orders
	ABC analyses	• Obsolete • Turnover rate	On request	On request	Production Logistics Accounting	Inventory postings
	Vendor rating	• Vendor selection	Monthly	Not available	Logistics	Inventory and invoice postings
	Stock level	• Monitoring • 'Free' stock • Not collected • Safety stocks • Classes	Weekly and monthly	Monthly	Production Logistics Accounting	Material master/inventory postings
	Delivery reliability	In terms of • Time • Quantity • Customer service	Weekly/monthly	Not available	Management Logistics	Deliveries/sales orders

Conclusions

- **SWOT analysis** This chapter contains the SWOT analysis of the to-be concept. It predicts not only the prospective weaknesses and threats but also the opportunities arising from the future organization, processes, and procedures. The SWOT analysis should not be focused exclusively on the software implementation but on the project as a whole, because certain SWOTs may be considered only after software implementation (e.g. re-engineering, organization).
- **Action list** The project management team proposes measures to be taken to tackle the key problems discussed in the previous chapter. The action list contains a number of areas where action has been proposed, usually by the steering committee but also possibly by other parties (see Table 7.1). The action list must be revised continually by the steering committee.

Appendices

All reports and forms used in the new environment have to be included in the appendices. Thus they are available for discussion purposes. The organizational charts, processes, and procedures of the new setup are likewise useful to have in the appendices. Illustrations are also useful for people outside the project.

Consequences of the to-be concept

Having established the as-is and to-be concepts, the differences between the two must be analyzed, and appropriate measures taken. As mentioned above, business process re-engineering (see Section 7.2) is useful only after introduction of the project, because only then is the full potential of the software understood. Nevertheless, minor adjustments in organization, processes, and procedures can be made during the project. This depends heavily on the availability of human resources, the expertise of the project teams, the attitude of the steering committee, and the company culture.

All weak points of the business processes should be recorded during the project itself in order to carry out business process re-engineering after implementation. BPR projects have to be planned and supervised by the steering committee.

4.6.3 Lessons learned for concepts

1. **Research the concept in depth and put it down in writing** The to-be concept is the basis and guideline for the whole project. All relevant matters concerning the future organization, processes,

procedures, and methods have to be discussed and investigated in depth and written down before starting with the realization phase. A clear and well-formulated concept protects the project team, promotes the project, and exposes any problems likely to arise during implementation.

2. **Invest the necessary time to create the concepts** The quality of the concepts depends on the capability and the time-input from the decision-makers. They have to be aware that the to-be concept will be central to the department in forthcoming years. Especially during the concept phase they have to make the necessary time available to work out a well-defined and high-quality concept. The better the to-be concept is formulated, the faster the progress in subsequent phases, because the necessary decisions concerning the future structures have been taken and agreed upon.

3. **Make the line manager responsible for the** concepts Line managers have to be fully involved in setting up the as-is and to-be concepts. For one reason, they know their departments best; for another reason, the to-be concept shapes the future of their departments. By collaborating on the concepts they will understand departmental processes and procedures in the future, and avoid losing touch.

4. **Highlight the importance of SWOT analysis** It is important to draw the project's attention to the SWOT analysis as an indication not only of predicted weaknesses and threats but also of potential opportunities in the future. The SWOT analysis should not be focused exclusively on the software implementation but on the project as a whole, because certain SWOTs may be considered only after software implementation. The SWOTs should be discussed and appropriate measures taken to guarantee a successful project implementation.

5. **Get approval for the concepts** All business concepts have to be known and approved by the project team, the line management, and the steering committee. This approval helps to insure the project team against repetitive, pointless, and controversial discussions, and enforces ownership on those who approved the concepts.

4.7 Technical environment

The technical environment describes the hardware configuration for the SAP application, the network infrastructure linking up all sales offices and plants, and the software purchase and programming constraints.

4.7.1 Hardware

We decided to install the hardware centrally in Lucerne, and serve all sales offices and plants via a wide area network (WAN). The hardware had to be set up in such a way that it did not become the bottleneck for the project.

It was particularly difficult to estimate the additional hardware needed for each module being implemented or for a release upgrade. Experience had shown that every major release change was likely to use more memory, disk space, or processor speed. We therefore tried to gather the necessary information in advance. Sources of information were the consulting company, SAP, and Early Watch from SAP. The best forecast could be given by Early Watch, as they knew our hardware environment best and had the most sophisticated tools for checking our requirements.

SAP server

We started with a Hewlett-Packard (HP) G30 for phase 1 of the project. We chose a UNIX operating system and an Oracle database since this was the most reliable choice at that time. Today, Windows NT is, of course, a good alternative.

One year later before going into production, we bought a second machine, an HP G50, which served the SD, FI, and MM modules. Furthermore we upgraded our test machine from an HP G30 to an HP G50 in order to provide enough power for the next project phases.

With the introduction of the PP and CO modules in both plants two years after project start, we again had to increase our computer power, and had to purchase an HP K200. The old production machine HP G50 became our test machine.

In the third project year we carried out a release change. The additional hardware required for this upgrade completely surprised us. We had had no previous indication from any side that the new release would need more internal memory. After the release change the machine was virtually unusable as the response times increased to minutes and hours. We urgently had to increase our memory and add an additional processor, which brought us back to more normal response times. Our machines are now equipped as follows:

- Production machine HP K200/2 with 2 GB memory and 54 GB of mirrored disk: that is 27 MB available for data storage.
- Test machine HP G50 with 768 MB memory and 21 GB of disk.

We do not work with an application server as our database servers have never been a bottleneck in our hardware configuration. Our disks are mirrored to secure the availability of data.

One test machine and one production machine have proved useful while in production. A single test machine is not adequate, however, in the event of a release upgrade. Two test machines are needed: one machine for installing and testing the new release; the second for developing and testing in the production environment, and also for transporting changes to the production machine.

WAN

Our wide area network is outsourced to Unisource Business Networks (see Figure 4.5). Unisource guarantees an availability of 99.8%. The network is supervised 24 hours a day, and any interruption is registered and communicated immediately. We had a good experience in outsourcing the WAN, with few network problems. The exception was the line to the Welsh plant, where owing to the poor telephone lines we had several very annoying breakdowns until eventually the line was completely replaced. After this experience, Unisource installed ISDN backup lines for additional security to head office and to both the Dutch and Welsh plants.

The WAN transmission rate was the bottleneck in our hardware configuration. We started with a transmission rate of 8 kbps and had to upgrade quickly to 16 kbps to ensure good response times in all sites. We even installed a 32 kbps line in our plants and head office.

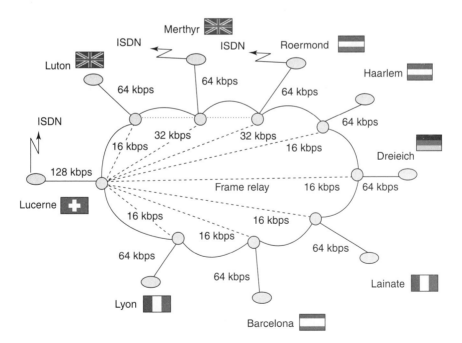

Figure 4.5   Wide area network design.

4.7.2   Software

Software purchase

We bought the complete SAP package with all modules included, since this was cheaper than buying every module separately. The whole package cost us in the region of SFr600,000. This price was rather high, especially for a medium-sized company. However, SAP now offers special packages for small and medium-sized companies through system houses. This amounts to SFr250,000 for a company of our size and even less for small companies (approximately SFr95,000 for a 15 user licence).

We decided to purchase the software in the Netherlands (where our plant is located) to get a better price than that available in Switzerland. The difference amounted to 10% at that time. Since then the price differences have leveled out.

Programming guidelines

Implementing a standard software package such as SAP offers a high degree of flexibility. Modifications to the standard software therefore should be disallowed, since the cost of such changes is enormous with each new software release. To prevent any such changes, our project strategy explicitly stated that all modifications required the steering committee's approval.

With this principle we managed to avoid any modification of the SAP standard program, but we could not prevent modifications due to program errors. Program errors in the SAP standard had to be corrected by our own programmers following correction notes from SAP. These correction notes were quite extensive. We treated them as modifications, and therefore they had to undergo the program request procedure as described in the following section.

In the meantime, SAP introduced hot-patch updates. Hot patches contain the latest program improvements and error corrections, and are sent to customers regularly. They should make it possible to reduce the volume of correction notes needed in the system.

Program request

On several occasions a user required an immediate program request, or one of our programmers changed a program without being aware of the consequences in other modules. Such fast changes often lead to problems afterwards because people do not think carefully about their program requirements.

To ensure optimal security and stability we had to set up a program request form. The program request form helps programmers to plan and reduce their workload. The applicants are forced to think carefully about their requests. The result is greater efficiency.

Our program request form principles were set up as follows:

1. All users requesting a new program or a program change had to fill in a program request form.
2. The form had to be approved by the line manager and sent to the project leader/module coordinator responsible.
3. The project leader/module coordinator gathered the detailed information necessary and decided on the request.
4. The programmer/analyst took over the responsibility for the program and contacted the user if more information was required.

Program changes

All program changes should follow the above procedure. If not, all changes must at least be approved by the program author and the module coordinator before releasing them into production. The change has to be documented in the program header and in those program lines modified, according to the example below:

```
*-------------------------------------------------*

Changes:


EL981209  add new selection criteria sales group


*-------------------------------------------------*

. . . . .
. . . . .
select * from ...                    "new EL981209
```

Naming conventions

We set up naming conventions for our programs (see Table 4.11). These mark them as customer-specific programs and identify the origin. The name length was eight digits, and each digit had a meaning.

Table 4.11 Naming conventions

Digit	Example	Explanation
1	Z	Z to identify the program as customer specific
2	S	Module identification: B = BC, S = SD, M = MM, P = PP, F = FI, C = CO, A = AM, H = HR
3, 4	SH	Module part, e.g. SH for shipping, BI for billing, OR for order etc.
5	C	Country where program has been developed: C = CH, N = NL, G = GB
6, 7, 8	001	Internal sequential numbering

4.7.3   Maintenance of hardware and software

Our system manager spends about 60% of his time in maintaining and supervising hardware and software environment.

Our hardware must be available 24 hours a day to allow a three-shift production in the plants. During the week we carry out on-line saves. On Saturday nights only, we shut down the machines for a few hours to allow an off-line save.

4.7.4   Lessons learned in the technical environment

1. **Design the hardware concept with enough reserves for future growth**   The hardware must be set up so that it does not become a bottleneck in the project. The additional hardware requirements must be known and installed before new modules go live or before a release upgrade. It is difficult to calculate the additional amount of hardware needed for each module to be implemented. Major releases will also require more memory, disk space, and processor speed.
2. **Install backup lines for important connections in the network**   It is advantageous to have the most important lines backed up with another line, ISDN for example. This should guarantee absolute security in a network.
3. **Avoid any standard software modifications**   Implementing a standard software package such as SAP already offers a high degree of flexibility. Modifications to the standard software afterwards should be disallowed since the maintenance and cost of such changes are enormous with each new software release. All proposed modifications should be approved by the steering committee.
4. **Set up programming guidelines and naming conventions**   Programming guidelines and naming conventions help to organize and control development activities. This can also offer additional security, since it helps to track the origin of a problem quickly.
5. **Insist on program applicants using program request forms**   Program request forms are helpful to organize and reduce the programmer's work. A program request form forces the applicant to think very carefully about a request. This enables the programmer to plan and work more efficiently.

5 Realization phase

The goal of the realization phase is to build up a system prototype reflecting all the company processes and procedures defined in the to-be concept. The main activities during this phase relate to customization: in other words, configuring the system tables according to the business requirements. Furthermore, reports and forms required by the company must be created, programmed conversion and interfaces, and authorizations set up. The realization and preparation phases overlap: that is, certain activities from the preparation phase take place simultaneously with others from the realization phase.

5.1 Model organizational structure

Before starting customization, it must be clear how to embed the company's organizational structure, processes, and procedures into the SAP system: that means having the to-be concept already prepared.

First, structures and procedures must be analyzed and then matched to the SAP structures. Modeling organizational structures is a fundamental step in the project. A lot of settings are difficult to change, or cannot be changed at all later on.

This step took us quite a while because our organizational structures and processes were not very clearly defined but had simply evolved gradually as the company expanded. After a lot of discussions with the people best acquainted with the department, the processes, or procedures (usually the line managers), we finally agreed on the to-be concept and set up the structure in the system accordingly.

Another problem we faced was the impact of our settings on other modules. The disadvantage of step-by-step implementation is the unavailability of the module specialists during the modeling phase. In our case we lacked knowledge of the production and planning module (PP) when implementing the previous modules. This left us a few tricky problems to solve in the PP environment.

This is the phase where good consultants are very valuable to the company – especially that rare species who is familiar with the links to other modules.

Today there are helpful tools available for gaining more insight into the software and company processes. This enables the company to map company processes against the appropriate SAP processes, and to see the impact of project implementation before anything is customized.

5.2 Customizing

SAP provides the implementation guide (IMG), which makes implementation as easy as possible. The IMG has a lot of useful and comprehensive functionality, which allows a fast customization. For each business application the IMG explains every step in the implementation process, explains the SAP standard setting, describes the system configuration work (activities), and opens the activities interactively. Although it requires discipline to work with this IMG, it is still worthwhile as you gain perfect control over the progress of the project.

SAP always delivers one example per organization unit (client 001). We strongly recommend using the standard setup for your own organization units and adapting the attributes to meet your requirements. This has the advantage that many tables are already customized in the system, thus considerably reducing the amount of time needed to configure the system.

5.3 Conversion and interfaces

5.3.1 Considerations for conversion and interfaces

The data conversion and interface to other programs or modules are certainly one of the most critical points in any project. Here also we learned something. Our data conversion in the material management area incorrectly transferred the data from our old computer system to the materials management module in SAP. Unfortunately we realized this only after production started, and had a lot of hassle and manual work to correct it.

Also, in the interface area in certain projects we experienced incorrect links to other modules, so that incorrect data was passed on to other modules (see also Section 10.2).

However, these were not the only projects with problems in this area. In almost all projects the conversion and interfaces were tackled too late.

Below are a few important points to take into consideration for conversion and interfaces:

- **High priority necessary** The importance of the conversion and interfaces is usually realized too late, since other direct project-related problems are given higher priority.

- **Conversion is time consuming**   The amount of time used for planning, programming, testing, and converting the data is often underestimated. It is important that the conversion and interface topic is already taken up in the planning phase of the project, and that the necessary preparations are initiated. The conversion and interfaces have to be fully programmed, planned, and tested during the realization phase. At the beginning of the preparation phase, the conversion and interface handbook should be ready, and the only work remaining should be the conversion run to the productive system and the data check by the project members.
- **Expert know-how needed**   Hire additional external consultants for programming the conversion and interfaces in case you run into a human resource bottleneck during the realization phase.
- **Data has to be tested by the user**   The conversion is not just an IT matter to be completed after the technical data transfer. The data has to be checked and tested after conversion by the project members and key users before it is released into production. The same is valid for interfaces: they have to be tested in advance to guarantee a correct data flow.
- **Plan the conversion**   The data conversion usually takes place on a weekend because the data must not be changed during the conversion. The people involved must be informed well in advance.
- **Set up a handbook**   A conversion and interface handbook helps to organize and control the conversion (see Section 5.3.3).
- **Check the quality of the old data**   The quality of the source data must be checked and corrected before it is transferred. Otherwise incorrect data might be transferred to the new system. We experienced incorrect data in the old system that had not been noticed by the user.
- **Consider manual data transfer**   If the source data is not at least 90% compliant with the SAP software standards, a manual transfer should be considered. Investigate very well the time needed for an automatic transfer. The writing of a conversion program, the conversion itself, and the control of the data are time consuming and often underestimated. Our experience was that manual data transfer is often faster than automated transfer.

5.3.2   Conversion and interface project

Conversion and interfaces are a very critical part of every project. However, they usually do not get the required attention from project leaders, mainly because they lack the necessary IT knowledge. We found it wise to create a separate subproject for the whole conversion and interface area. The conversion and interface project must, of course, be in line with the main project, and is directly controlled by the project manager.

Table 5.1 Contents of conversion and interface handbook

1. Conversion and interface scope
    1.1 Definition
    1.2 Objectives
    1.3 Strategy
2. Project organization
    2.1 Organizational chart
    2.2 Human resources
    2.3 Tasks and responsibilities
3. Conversion and interface details
    3.1 Description of conversion
    3.2 Data-volume calculation
    3.3 Description of interfaces
4. Implementation schedule
5. Project activities
    5.1 Reporting
    5.2 Meetings
    5.3 Standards
6. Controlling and security

Setting up the conversion and interfaces as a separate project has the advantage that this project has to fulfill all requirements of a normal project:

- The IT members become the owners of the project and take over full responsibility for it.
- A handbook describing all the steps of the conversion must be produced (see Section 5.3.3).
- An implementation schedule guarantees detailed planning of all activities and human resources involved.
- The reporting allows the project management to monitor and co-ordinate progress.

5.3.3   Conversion and interface handbook

To get a better insight into conversion and interfaces, it is necessary to produce a conversion and interface handbook containing the information listed in Table 5.1.

5.4   Forms and reports

5.4.1   Forms

The necessary time to establish the forms and the appropriate print output was underestimated in all projects. The creation of forms is not critical as long as it does not concern external papers such as invoices.

The following critical points have to be considered for setting up the forms:

1. Get user requirements.
2. Customize the form (set up the right parameters).
3. Program the form (adjust to company standards).
4. Create print output.
5. Get user acceptance.

Customizing

The customizing of the printed forms is an important matter, because the forms are being sent to the customer or supplier. If the invoices are not ready by project start-up, no money will be paid, or in the supplier's case the wrong goods will be delivered. Two things should be considered in order to avoid wasting time:

- The user acceptance procedure for external forms is a time-consuming process, because these documents represent the company to the customer. Marketing find it difficult to adapt to a different invoice format.
- Production of the forms is very technically demanding where the standard form is not used. In most cases, Marketing will not be satisfied with the standard form, since they prefer to have their own, company-specific image.

Programming the form

A standard form is delivered by SAP. As long as this form is used with few changes, the programming effort can be minimized. However, for most companies this form does not suit their needs. They want to have a special market image, or a form that suits their internal needs. This means that the form has to be created from scratch, which requires special expertise.

Print output

Customizing and programming are the first steps toward creation of a form. Another difficult and time-consuming step is the alignment of the form to the printers. This was difficult in several projects. Hence having the same brand of printer throughout the company is a big advantage when customizing.

5.4.2 Reports

Reporting needs

A lot of standard reports are available in SAP for every module, and generally cover all requirements. SAP offers a variety of easy tools for creating reports. Key users can use these tools to create their own reports. More sophisticated reports need to be created by IT specialists with SAP program expertise.

Nevertheless, we had to adapt a lot of reports to our needs because our users requested the information in a way that was convenient for them, or perhaps the report just had to look like the one they were used to. In any case, reporting is a very company-specific matter as well as being a key point for user acceptance of the system.

Reports are an important tool, especially for enabling the management to run the company. It is therefore necessary to discuss the reporting requests thoroughly in the to-be concept to make sure all needs are covered. In spite of the to-be concept we found that a lot of requests for new reports or for changes were made after introduction, because it was precisely then that people realized what figures were really needed and, of course, were needed fast.

With this in mind, it is wise to plan enough IT capacity after introduction to cover the report requests.

Report-request form

Although we are not a big company, we created a report-request form and set up an administrative procedure for the following reasons:

- To fill in a report-request form is time consuming, and consequently people carefully consider the real need for the request before making it.
- The request must be approved by the line manager to verify the need for the report.
- IT people can plan their work, and do not have constantly to work on rush orders.
- Reporting needs are programmed faster because there is an organized way of working.
- People like a systematic method for handling their requests.
- Report requests can be coordinated among the different companies, thus preventing duplicate reports being programmed in various sites.

5.5　Authorization

SAP is a completely integrated system. It can provide an immense amount of information about all business processes of a company. On the one hand the information must be reliable, and therefore data entries and changes must be controlled; on the other hand access to sensitive data must be restricted.

Consequently, an authorization concept is needed. The creation of an authorization concept for a specific module is time consuming because it has to be set up and approved by the line manager and customized by the IT people. Neither of these activities is easy to carry out.

Line managers must define the access rights of their staff. Such access rights must be formulated in terms of transactions. For this task, line managers need the support of a project management team member, who can explain to them the consequences of every transaction.

The customizing of the authorization request in the SAP system is not an easy task, and must be done by experienced IT staff. For security reasons only one IT person per site was responsible for customizing the authorizations.

Responsibility for authorization rests squarely with the line whereas customizing is a matter for the IT personnel.

To have a basis for customizing and obtaining the official approval of the line managers, we issued an authorization request form (see Appendix, Figure A.10) to be filled in by the applicant.

5.6 Prototyping

The goal of this phase is to prepare a test system for initial user demonstrations. All processes must be customized, and reliable test data must be made available. The key users have to check the system flows; print reports and forms; test the authorizations; and give their feedback to project members.

Prototyping theoretically should take place at the end of the realization phase. In practice, this interaction between project team and user is an ongoing process during the whole realization phase. As soon as the project team has a task finished in the project (a report, a specific flow, a form, etc.), they contact the user to get feedback on the work done. At the end of the realization phase it still is helpful to spend a day or two with the user to carry out a complete test of the whole customized module.

5.7 Lessons learned for realization phase

1. **Build a prototype** The goal for the realization phase is to build up a prototype containing the main processes and procedures of the business module and appropriate test data. The prototype has to be discussed with the key users, and provides initial feedback from the line organization to the project team.

2. **Check integration with other business modules** Customizing a business module starts with some basic organizational structures, which might also be valid for other modules. As some basic settings cannot be changed later on, it is important to consider the impact of the settings, and make sure the integration of other

modules is not impeded. The business module settings have to be discussed with people from the respective departments. Those people may have to work with the information from this module.

3. **Plan the conversions and interfaces well and in time** The conversion and interfaces have to be ready in time to enable the transfer and verification of the data. The amount of time used for planning, programming, converting, and testing the data is often underestimated. Missing or incorrect data may delay or even jeopardize the project. It is important that the conversion and interface areas be considered in the planning phase, and programmed and tested in the realization phase. The conversion is not just an IT matter that is completed after the technical data transfer. The data has to be checked and tested after conversion by the project members and key users before it is signed off for use in production.

4. **Remember that the procedure to create the forms is time consuming** The user procedure and programming for external forms are time consuming, since such documents represent the company image to the customer, and also require specific programming expertise. In order to have the forms ready by project start-up, they have to be discussed and settled with the user in the realization phase.

5. **Ensure good consultancy for the start-up phase** A good external consultant can help you a lot in the initial stages of customizing. In this first phase it is especially important that the external consultant advises in the customization, thus avoiding incorrect initial settings. The customizing should also be documented for later use by the company.

6 Preparation phase

This is the phase for going live and for handing the system over to line management. During this phase the production system has to be customized, the integration and quality tests have to be carried out in the production environment, and the data has to be converted from the old to the new system. The data transfer to the productive system is without doubt the most difficult and critical issue at this stage. It must be carried out shortly before going live, and because there is little time for correcting errors at this stage, it must have been thoroughly prepared during the realization phase.

It is also important that the users have been well trained to enforce ownership of the system, and that all the appropriate documentation has been completed before handover.

6.1 User manual and support

6.1.1 User manual

The user manual serves as a training handbook, as system documentation, and ultimately as a daily reference resource. A good manual promotes user acceptance of the software. It should be ready before the training begins so that people can familiarize themselves with its use, adding personal remarks as appropriate.

If this is not the case, the likelihood that the manual will remain unused is high, since quick reference is not possible by those unfamiliar with the document.

We found that documenting the system and writing the user manual are often neglected since nobody wants to take responsibility for these tasks. Consequently it is advisable to assign responsibility specifically to a particular person. That individual then assumes ownership of the manual, and is responsible for the following tasks:

- Setting standards for the manual.
- Collaborating with the other project members to produce it.
- Coordinating the information with other modules.
- Keeping the manual updated once the major changes to the system have gone through and processes have been altered.

The manual must be revised, supplemented, and improved from time to time, and with this in mind its structure should be kept as flexible as possible. In this way, chapters can be easily amended and/or expanded subsequently. Above all, the user manual should be user-friendly: that is, as simple and concise as possible.

Responsibility for the manual clearly carries with it a role in training the users. The person allocated that responsibility and role naturally will be identified by the users as their expert adviser, and as such will provide the 'internal hotline' (see next section).

6.1.2   User support

The concept of a hotline or competence centre is potentially very attractive to users. It is certainly important that they know where they can get help, particularly after a module has gone into production.

The downside of hotlines, however, is their negative influence on user behavior. Secure in the knowledge of instant support, the user's first reflex is to pick up the phone – even for the most minor problems, which could be solved easily by consulting the manual. The normal learning process is suspended indefinitely, as problem solving is delegated almost entirely to the on-line service. Demand for the service increases, consuming valuable human resources that otherwise could be deployed in core business activities.

We drew the following conclusions:

- Resources are better invested in producing a high-quality manual than in manning a continuous hotline with highly qualified staff.
- Most user problems do not require urgent attention, and will often work themselves out, given time.
- It should not be made too easy for users to get through to the hotline.
- Hotline personnel should not be too approachable. They must discourage routine contacts.

6.2   Archiving

6.2.1   Archiving tool

We needed a system with archiving and storage capacity for SAP data (from our central database and system management in Lucerne) and also for non-SAP documents (mainly drawings and designs from the development and maintenance departments at our plants).

Our specifications were that it should:

- Offer easy archiving and retrieval facilities for data and documents.
- Provide fast access to archived material.

- Give decentralized access to the material.
- Also allow us to archive non-SAP documents.
- Guarantee a high degree of security.
- Comply with legal regulations.

SAP offers a standard package for archiving data only, not documents.

The SAP-related company IXOS, on the other hand, satisfied all of our criteria for both data and document archiving. Their system is completely integrated into the workflow. The documents are easy to retrieve, and are accessible on-line. As a costly disadvantage, the IXOS solution required the purchase of additional hardware and software. The IXOS software cost about SFr100,000 for 150 users and the hardware (server, scanner, optical-disk unit) another SFr70,000.

Following a systems study for the Swiss headquarters by IXOS consultants, we reached the sobering conclusion that:

- Archiving data would save only about 200 MB per month.
- The IXOS archiving capacity would be excessive for the amount of data used at the headquarters.

On the basis of this honest consultancy, we decided to archive our SAP data at the headquarters using the SAP standard tools with disks. Purchasing additional disks was a cheaper alternative to investing in the IXOS hardware.

On the other hand, IXOS technology was necessary for document archiving at our Dutch plant, which required a document management system for the following reasons:

- They have a legal obligation to store a large number of documents, such as orders, delivery notes, and invoices.
- Various departments needed storage for non-SAP documents such as designs and drawings.
- They needed decentralized, fast, and easy access to all the data.

6.2.2 On-line availability of data

The rules governing availability of data vary according to the domestic legal requirements of each country. Usually the data must be stored for an average of 10 years. The on-line availability of data, however, can be determined by the line manager. This was fixed by our own line managers as follows:

- Sales orders: 6 months
- Deliveries: 6 months
- Sales invoices: 24 months
- Production orders: 12 months
- Finance documents: 24 months

6.3   Integration test

All testing, whether for integration or for migration, must be thoroughly prepared and seriously carried out. A time schedule (see Appendix, Figure A.12) and a test plan (see Appendix, Figure A.11) provide the necessary time and functional controls. It pays to spend sufficient time in preparing this test phase.

Time schedule   We determined the time schedule in the same way as the implementation schedule (see Section 4.5). The time schedule describes the sequence and the time frame of all tasks to be done during the test phase. We again used Microsoft Project as our planning tool, with columns for task, start, estimated finish, actual finish, resources, and comments.

Test plan   The test plan must cover all functions of a module. As a checklist it must describe all activities exhaustively and in detail. We listed all transactions, tables, forms, reports, menus, authorizations, master data, etc. The links to other modules also must be assured and tested.

6.4   Data transfer

As already mentioned in Section 5.3, data transfer is a crucial aspect of the project. Most of the problems we encountered after introduction of a module were always related to incorrect data transfers or interfaces.

Below are a few considerations that should be taken into account (along with those itemized in Section 5.3):

- The data transfer must be given a high priority.
- It is a time-consuming process, and sufficient time must be set aside not only for the technical data transfer but also for checking it afterwards.
- The transferred data must be fully tested in every detail by the line organization whose data it is.
- The transfer should be done at the latest possible moment in order to keep manual transfer to the minimum.
- The people involved must be given sufficient warning so that they can work at weekends or late nights.
- The data transfer needs to be coordinated with the other modules that might also require weekend working before going live.

6.5   Going live preparation

6.5.1   Start date

Various factors influence the start-up of a module. We made distinctions based on the amount of data and the time of year.

Choosing the start date according to the amount of data for transfer:

- For finance-related modules such as FI and CO, it is an advantage to start at the beginning of the company's accounting year in order to have balanced and settled accounts.
- For sales-related modules such as sales and distribution and material management, it is advisable to start at a time when orders are low so as to avoid having to process large numbers of open orders and deliveries.
- Production-related modules can usually start at any time of the year; advisable, however, is a period with a low order income.

Choosing the start date according to the time of year:

- The Christmas and New Year period offers the advantage that the data is more static and, for example, can be transferred more easily by the project team.
- To start during the summer break brings the advantage of low orders when going live, and this allows more time for correcting errors.
- Of course, both the above options have the drawback for project members that they must take their holidays at another time.

6.5.2   Project member preparation

Depending on how preparations are progressing, the project members have to be on call for weekend and late-night working at least two weeks before and two weeks after going live. Their personal and holiday agenda must conform with this.

6.5.3   Technical preparation

Hardware preparation

Before a module is put into production, an estimate must be made of the additional disk capacity and CPU power required. This must be done at least two months in advance, as the delivery of disks and CPUs always takes time. If additional disk space is ordered, the capacity of the backup tapes must also be considered. DAT tapes with about 6 GB per tape were too slow and unreliable for the required data volume. We soon changed to DLT technology (20–40 GB).

For us, the most important factor in the hardware infrastructure is the wide area network (see Section 4.7.1), because the transmission speed is often the bottleneck in the whole hardware setup. The WAN has to be capable of guaranteeing good response times in all attached locations. An increase of the overall transmission rate has to be considered early enough, as the procedure for increasing the rate takes weeks!

Software preparation

Before going into production, a client copy must always be transferred from the live to the test system. This ensures that the test and live system have almost the same data on-line. If there are problems after going live, the person responsible for the module can reconstruct them in the test environment and give a rapid response without disturbing the live system.

The closer to start-up that the client copy is made, the better the quantity and quality of data after it. Nevertheless, a safety margin must be built in, allowing recall of the client copy in case the first one fails, for whatever reason.

The disk space requirements are constantly monitored in the test and live systems so that an accurate estimate is provided of the required space in the test machine before the client copy is made.

System maintenance must be planned well enough in advance, because it is always weekend work. IT staff must also arrange their personal lives accordingly.

6.6   Lessons learned for preparation phase

1. **Prepare the user documentation well in advance**   This makes a valuable contribution to training and user acceptance, but its contribution will be diminished if it is not ready before training begins. Resources are better invested in producing a high-quality manual than in manning a continuous hotline with highly qualified staff.

2. **Prepare the data transfer to the live system carefully**   The data transfer to the productive system must be planned in detail. The data transfer is critical, because it usually takes place just before going live, and that leaves no time to repeat the whole process in the event of failure. The time available for transferring data is limited. Therefore the IT staff, who make the transfer, as much as the project members, who test the data, must make the best use of that time.

3. **Choose the right start date**   Putting a module into production must be coordinated with the line business. It should interfere as little as possible with normal, day-to-day business, and consequently should be scheduled for a period of low activity. Potential constraints on the implementation schedule must also be considered: the finance module, for example, needs to be implemented at the start of the financial year to maintain balanced and settled accounts.

4.   **Warn project team members about the forthcoming stress period** Project members and key users should be aware of the heavy workload they will face both before and after going live. Their personal interests must take second place at these times.

7 Productive phase

In this phase the line organization must take over the ownership of the implemented system. Meanwhile the project team have to adjust and fine-tune the system. They must conclude the business process re-engineering and follow-up projects and assess their results. These projects focus mainly on adapting the organization to the newly implemented software while improving its processes and procedures. Therefore business process re-engineering and follow-up projects are necessary to bring the whole project to a successful conclusion.

7.1 Optimize system

After implementation, the project team will be busy with actively adapting and fine-tuning the system. Optimizing the system is needed since not all business scenarios can be fully tested until they are in their real environment. Also in many cases the users realize their actual requirements only when the system is up and running.

We found that most customizing was set up well, and only minor adjustments were necessary. This is thanks to thorough research of the as-is and the to-be concepts, skillful transports, and good consulting.

Further adaptations and even new programs for reports and forms will be requested as soon as users realize just how much information can be retrieved from their new system.

The required time to stabilize the system varies from project to project depending heavily on the project setup. There are various factors that may influence the time needed to stabilize the system:

- **Data conversion and transfer** (see Section 6.4) If data is not converted correctly, problems will inevitably occur, and will seriously affect the implementation.
- **System test and preparation** Sufficient time must be set aside to carry out a thorough system test and to prepare the system.

- **To-be concept** It is important for the project to co-develop the to-be concept with line personnel. This avoids surprises during and after project implementation.
- **User training and information** If the users are well trained and informed about the project they will be able to solve problems independently.

7.2 Business process re-engineering (BPR)

During the project implementation, minor adaptations of the organization, processes, and procedures are required so that they conform to the standard software. The full business process re-engineering described in this section, by contrast, involves major changes in these areas, and should be carried out after, rather than before or during, the project implementation.

7.2.1 BPR after project implementation

The first step for project management is to implement the IT system successfully and on time. The second is to meet all of the objectives set at the beginning of a project; this may even be a more crucial factor.

The company has to improve and adapt its organization, processes, and procedures to the standard software. By implementing an integrated software package such as SAP, the IT environment is upgraded (see also Section 7.2.2). However, all other business management elements, processes, organization, methods, and procedures cannot be improved so quickly. As most of the management goals set for a project concern the three latter elements, subsequent projects must ensure that these objectives are achieved.

We are convinced that business process re-engineering has to be conducted after the project implementation of an enterprise resource planning package, for the following reasons:

- Business process re-engineering requires good knowledge of the enterprise resource planning package to reorganize business processes to conform to the integrated standard software processes. As the total functionality and potential of the software is only fully appreciated after implementation of the software, it is inadvisable to reorganize before implementation.
- BPR during the SAP implementation is likely to fail, because a combination of an IT system change with BPR will exceed the capacity of most employees to absorb the changes (see Section 8.4).

- Complexity is reduced, because organization, processes, and procedures are determined by the standard software.
- Capable human resources from the project with the requisite knowledge of processes are more readily available after project implementation.
- BPR is a highly political matter as it affects people's livelihood and professional status. Raising such political issues before project implementation is risky because it is bound to provoke strong reactions from those concerned and could create very unfavourable conditions for the subsequent SAP project.

7.2.2 Elements of business management

Implementing a software package such as SAP R/3 has an enormous impact on any company. The business processes, procedures, and entire organization must be brought into line with the software. These changes are not merely in the IT area; they have even wider implications in the other business areas. Introducing SAP will transform the IT environment to a highly sophisticated level, leaving other elements of the business behind.

To get the full benefits of the package and eventually to improve effectiveness and efficiency throughout the whole company, it is necessary to align and balance all of the four basic elements – processes, organization, methods and procedures, and information technology (see Figure 7.1).

With the implementation of our SAP project we improved the IT environment and partially adapted the organization, processes, procedures, and

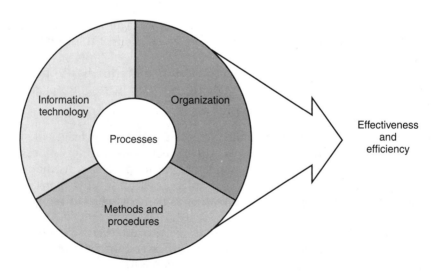

Figure 7.1 Elements of business management.

methods. The aim of the post-project activities described in Section 7.2.3 is to improve further these elements of business management and to integrate them with information technology.

Here are some considerations to be taken into account in each of the four basic elements of business management:

- Processes:
  - These should be simple, straightforward, and reliable.
  - Processes must be at the heart of every to-be concept.
  - All procedural changes must be discussed and approved by the steering committee.
- Organization:
  - A good organization assigns the right job to the right person.
  - Authority, tasks, and responsibilities should be clearly defined and allocated.
  - Job profiles and descriptions should be used to clarify structures and responsibilities.
- Methods and procedures:
  - Methods and procedures must be adapted according to the product/ market.
  - They must conform to customer requirements.
- Information technology:
  - The system should be fully exploited.
  - Using the system to its full potential should produce faster and more comprehensive management information.

7.2.3   Business process re-engineering projects

Weak points in business processes must be identified during implementation of the enterprise resource planning package so that they can be covered in the subsequent BPR.

The project management must initiate BPR projects and pass them over to the line organization whose processes and procedures they affect. However, these line projects still fall under the umbrella of the total project implementation, and so the project manager is still jointly responsible for them, and should take an active role in their implementation.

During the project we kept an 'open issue list' (see Table 7.1). The open issue list contained a number of activities where action was required by the project team, the line organization, or the steering committee. The action list was set up based on the to-be concept and problems occurring during the project. The action list had to be carried out under the supervision of the steering committee, because these issues were mainly conducted as BPR projects.

Table 7.1 Open issue list

Issue	Responsible	Deadline
1. Define customer matrix	HK	30.09.98
2. Define performance measures	SC	31.10.98
3. Reduce amount of self-collectors	HK	31.03.98
4. Clarify definition of functions and tasks	VE	31.12.98
5. Set up activity plan for lead-time reduction	VE, HK	01.07.98
6. Investigate allocation policy	HK, VE	31.12.98
7. Lower stock situation	VE	31.12.98
8. Reduce start-up losses	VE, HE	31.12.99
9. Decrease number of cores	VE, HK	30.09.99
10. Planning for foaming and cross-linking	VE	30.06.99
11. Investigate and improve supply-chain management	VE, HK	31.12.00
12. Evaluate process for small orders	VE, PK	31.12.00

The following sections explain the projects listed in Table 7.1.

Project 1: Define customer matrix

The aim of this project was to define a customer matrix. The customer matrix (see, for example, Table 7.2) defines the customer lead-time and service level. The customer lead-time is defined as the time between customer order entry and delivery. The service level indicates the quality of delivery. A service level of 90% means that 10 out of every 100 customer orders may be delivered early, late, or with a 10% variation in quantity.

Since SAP is an integrated software package, we had to define the lead-times and service level when customizing our system. The customer matrix is the basis for our logistics concept, and therefore a condition for Project 2 and Project 5.

Prior to the introduction of SAP, no systematic performance measures had been used in Plant or Sales. Neither Sales and Marketing nor the plants themselves really understood the mechanism of the customer matrix before it was discussed. The customer matrix issue provoked a detailed discussion between Plant and Sales about customer lead-times and service levels.

Table 7.2 Customer matrix for ALVEOLIT

ALVEOLIT	Lead-time 1 (weeks)	Service level 1 (%)	Lead-time 2 (weeks)	Service level 2 (%)
A. Sports – leisure	3	90	4	99
B. Shoes	3	90	4	99
C. Transportation	2	99	–	–
D. Construction	3	90	4	99
E. Manufacturing	3	90	4	99
F. Government	3	90	4	99
G. Buoyancy	3	90	4	99
H. Packaging	3	90	4	99
I. Adhesive tapes	3	90	4	99
K. Medical/orthopedic	3	90	4	99

The customer matrix was then checked against the empirical data available. This revealed discrepancies, and the matrix was adjusted accordingly. For example, performance measurements in the automotive sector varied between the matrix and our empirical data: the matrix indicated a lead-time of between 4 and 6 weeks where the empirical data placed it at between 1 and 2 weeks.

To obtain more precise data we needed to track performance measurements over several months. This produced some surprising figures for the service levels in our three product lines.

The basic outcome can be summarized as follows:

- ALVEOLIT: 90% service level reached after 6 weeks.
- ALVEOLEN: 90% service level reached after 4 weeks.
- ALVEOLUX: 90% service level reached after $7\frac{1}{2}$ weeks.

According to the customer matrix, Sales required a service level of 99% within 4 weeks. The steering committee agreed with the proposal that ALVEOLIT and ALVEOLEN reach a service level of 99% with a 4 week lead-time. The 4 week delivery period required by Sales had the consequences described in Project 5.

This customer matrix project certainly taught us a few lessons:

- No systematic performance measurements for our customer lead-times and service levels had been used in our Plant and Sales departments.
- Our assumption concerning customer lead-times and service levels were far from reality. We had a lot to improve.
- Commercial discussion between Plant and Sales improved with the more reliable data.
- Using empirical data to back up customer demands is more difficult.
- Reaction time is crucial for customer satisfaction.

Project 2: Define performance measurements

SAP offered us more information and opportunities to control our performance. The goal for this project was to define new performance measurements. We used performance measurements to monitor progress of the processes and to verify targets.

Our main performance measurements as defined in the customer matrix are as follows:

- Actual date of shipment against confirmed delivery date.
- Requested delivery date against confirmed delivery date.
- Lead-time by segment and product line.
- Requested, manufactured, and shipped quantity against requested quantity.

Project 3: Reduce amount of self-collectors

Self-collectors are customers who store their material at our site and make their own arrangements for transport from our plant to their premises. We faced the problem that our customers used our plant as a kind of storage area and caused us high stock costs. The goal was to lower the storage capacity by at least 50% with customer agreement. Intense negotiations with our customers helped us to achieve the goal within a short period.

This project clearly demonstrates how quickly a problem can be solved, given the right encouragement from the steering committee.

Project 4: Clarify definition of functions and tasks

With the introduction of SAP, certain processes and procedures changed. As a consequence, job profiles had to be sharpened up or rewritten. This item has been taken off the list, because the appropriate manager is attempting to solve the problem on a bilateral basis. The project is still pending.

We realized that all projects no longer supervised run a high risk of deteriorating because the necessary pressure and control are missing. Especially for projects where top managers are involved, it is vital to keep the pressure and control on the projects, because these managers are enormously busy and often set priorities according to pressure.

Project 5: Set up activity plan for lead-time reduction

The goal of the lead-time reduction project was to reduce the lead-time and bring the current 8 week lead-time down to that required by the customer (see Table 7.2).

Investigations on measures to shorten the lead-time showed the following results:

- **Reduction of the lot size**   The lot size will decrease by 11.4%. As a result, start and stop losses on the foaming ovens will increase by the same amount.
- **Increase total time of change over**   A considered estimate is that the time will increase by 25%. As a result, the start and stop losses for extruders will increase by 25%.
- **Financial impact yield**   The total yield loss will increase by 286,500 guilders.

The steering committee decided to accept the yield loss in order to shorten the lead-times.

Project 6: Investigate allocation policy

With the introduction of the PP module we gained new opportunities for controlling the system's allocation of material. The goal was to investigate these new possibilities and check their feasibility for our production system.

The investigation concluded that there was no need for additional allocation tools at that time. The existing allocation system was proven adequate. The sales operation planning tool will be considered at a later stage.

Project 7: Decrease stock

One of the major goals of the implementation in production was to lower the stocks in our Dutch plant: not only raw materials but also, and especially, finished products. At the time our production module went live, the stock level stood at 500 tons. Then it dropped to 300 tons, and currently it has leveled out at about 400 tons.

We achieved a 20% stock reduction with the following measures:

- Introduction of the make-to-order philosophy (see Section 10.4).
- Control of the self-collector stock (see Project 3).
- Improved control by the system.
- Reorganization of large and small orders.
- Reorganization of the raw material stock.
- Changing existing procedures for stocks controlled centrally from Head Office.

The most marked improvement was in the raw material stock. This was achieved by the following measures:

- **Inscribing cards on the raw material racks** This measure gave us reliable information about material that had been removed from the rack without completing proper administration.
- **Tracing back errors** Many small mistakes have been detected by this method. General awareness of problems has increased, and as a result human error has declined and the whole process has focused minds.
- **Introducing 'Place Kanban' for delivery to production** This system has proven to be simple and clear – almost foolproof.
- **Recording milling losses** This highlighted the differences between granulate and powder silos.
- **Physically separating storage areas** A clear and visible separation of storage areas or locations avoids mistakes.
- **Comparing particular raw materials on a daily basis** Such comparison highlights production corrections.

Project 8: Reduce start-up losses

In order to create more flexibility we focused on the reduction of start-up losses. The goal for this project was to eliminate the yield consequences of more frequent size changes and smaller production runs on the different machines in our process.

We took the following measures when investigating start-up losses:

- We recorded work processes on video.
- We split up the processes into separate stages.
- We measured the time for each stage.
- We discussed potential improvements.

Numerous causes of start-up losses were identified. Many of these were related to the die and to the working method. To start with, we focused on these two items:

- We developed an improved working method.
- We investigated the usage of a flexible die.

Project 9: Decrease number of cores

We have handled about 500 different core material numbers for our foam rolls. Planning and control of these numerous core material numbers was time consuming and expensive. The goal for this project was to decrease the number of cores by 50%.

The project team together with our customers investigated a suitable solution for standard thickness and length. The result so far has been a decrease of core material numbers from 500 to 280.

Core-cutting machines were evaluated. A new core-cutting machine would be less labor intensive, but not much quicker. We decided to purchase a core-cutting machine when the current one needs to be replaced for technical reasons.

With the reduction of the numbers of cores the stock control was simplified.

Project 10: Planning for foaming and cross–linking

To reduce the throughput times, planning needed to be improved. The goal for this project was to produce all foaming production orders within two days after extrusion. After investigating the planning process, the following changes were successfully implemented:

- Planners plan only the first production step (extrusion).
- The second and third production steps (cross-linking and foaming) are done by the respective departments.

The cross-linking and foaming departments were very skeptical at first about self-planning. Today they would miss the flexibility and independence it offers. They are currently very satisfied with the clear production overview available to them.

Project 11: Investigate and improve supply-chain management

Supply-chain management includes the control of the order management process not only with our customers but also with our suppliers. It requires better insight into the order and planning systems of all companies involved in the chain. The main benefits are better controlled stocks, lower stocks in the chain, and less disturbance in the total supply chain. The end results are lower overall costs and a lead-time consistent with market requirements.

This project has been started with some of our major customers. Open and honest discussions will bring, to all involved, a reduction in logistics costs and an improvement in service levels (we define the service level as a balance of required lead-time and delivery reliability).

Project 12: Evaluate process for small orders

Within our production processes we have insufficient flexibility for smaller orders. The reasons for this are as follows:

- Dedicated machines for certain products and product groups.
- Large product range.
- Time-intensive changeover between different production runs.
- Fixed processes.
- Human resources allocated to certain processes on a fixed basis.

In order to be able to react better to market requirements we had to create more overall flexibility, not only in machinery but also in personnel.

7.3   Follow-up projects

Standard software is mostly incapable of supporting all company-specific processes and procedures. SAP is continuously developing its software and adjusting it to market needs. As soon as all the modules are implemented, new versions of the software are available and, with it, new functionality.

The project management team and, in particular, the module co-ordinators have to know the improvements in the next releases for their modules. By introducing our modules we were aware of the improvements in the coming release. We constantly recorded follow-up projects to complete our implementation, to improve our processes and procedures, and to make our users' lives easier. After implementation of all SAP modules we planned about 20 follow-up projects. Table 7.3 shows examples from follow-up projects without going into detail.

Follow-up projects are often pushed into the background. We found that the follow-up projects in general got less attention as people got tired of

Table 7.3 Follow-up projects

Module	Project	Description
1. BC	Release change	Prepare the migration on the test and productive machine
1. BC	Introduce document management system	Link several document types to SAP objects: working instructions, drawings, CSS documents, product specifications, customer purchase orders
2. BC	Classification system	Improve setup and usage with regard to material master
3. BC	ALVEO operations information system	Catalog of all statistics required and used throughout ALVEO, irrespective of module
4. SD	Consignment flow	Redefine consignment flow; make correct consignment flow possible within the make-to-order flow
5. CO/PA	Improvement of budget functions	Shortcomings of the actual release to be corrected and possible improvements to be installed (such as link to sales orders, link to SOP)
6. FI/CO	Automatic payment of invoices	Automatic payment of *all* invoices: two payment runs per week
7. FI/CO	Electronic bank payments	Connection with banks regarding all postings. Introduce electronic banking in relation with SAP
8. MM	Redefine warehouse management	Optimize usage of warehouse management
9. MM	Transcargo using warehouse management	Link Transcargo to our system
10. MM	Automatic goods receipt after production order confirmation	Introduce this function
11. MM	Purchasing extension	Extend scope with transport and services, including invoice verification
12. PP	Mass replace function BOM	Introduce this function
13. PP	Discontinuation BOM	Introduce this function
14. PP	Batch number management	Investigate possibilities of changing the batch number for finished products
15. PUR	Plant-wide purchasing	Introduction of plant-wide replenishment function for both plants
16. PUR	Company-wide purchasing	Introduction of company-wide replenishment function (Italy/Spain and plants)
17. BC	Archiving/WFM	Introduce IXOS archiving system for data
18. FI/CO	Cash management treasury	Introduce new functionality
19. MM	Export documents	Implement standard documents from SAP
20. PP	Capacity leveling	Implement detailed scheduling
21. PP	Rough cut capacity planning	Implement RCCP via SOP, rolling sales plan
22. ALL	Small improvements	Test and if OK install improved module functions

project work. It is essential to plan the projects early enough and use the momentum of the project implementation to launch them and provide the basis for well-planned post-implementation projects.

7.4 Lessons learned for the productive phase

1. **Fulfill the project objectives** The productive phase ends the IT system implementation but not the whole program. To achieve the program objectives, the organization, processes, and procedures have to be improved with follow-up and business re-engineering projects.
2. **Initiate business process re-engineering (BPR) projects after system implementation** Business process re-engineering has to be conducted after and not before or during the system implementation. Doing the business process re-engineering before SAP implementation is inadvisable since the functionality and potential of the software can only be fully appreciated after implementation. Political disputes arising from BPR could also bring the whole project to a standstill or create very unfavorable conditions for the subsequent SAP project.
3. **Avoid conducting other large projects in parallel to the SAP project** The implementation of SAP software demands a lot of skilled human resources from the company. It is not viable to maintain several major projects successfully alongside regular line work. It is preferable to concentrate on one large project at a time and do it right. Too many parallel projects during the IT system implementation are likely to fail because people will be overwhelmed by conflicting demands.
4. **Be ready for a lengthy program of structural change** The implementation of the IT system is just the first step toward improving the organization. All other business processes have to be brought up to the same level, which will take some time and effort. It is important to plan the projects early enough and use the momentum of the project implementation to get the follow-up projects started right after the system implementation.
5. **Hand the project over to the line organization** The implemented project has to be handed over to the line organization so they can take over the ownership of the implemented system. They have to maintain and improve the system according to their needs.

8 Overall project phases

Training, project control, risk management, and change management are issues that affect all phases of the project.

Training starts with education of the project team in system, line, and project management, and ends with the training of the users.

Project control is carried out during the whole project according to the project-controlling cycle. The project team has to measure and identify constantly any deviation from the project schedule.

Risk management is also an activity to be pursued during the whole project by all project members. Potential risks need to be identified at an early stage and analyzed properly, and preventive measures need to be initiated to avoid them.

The changes perceived during implementation must be actively managed to guide those affected through negative and positive cycles.

8.1 Training

Training constitutes one of the most important and difficult tasks in any project. It is difficult because each user group (project members, key users, management, production operators, etc.) has different needs, preferences, and learning potential, and they must be trained at different phases of the project.

The project members are also in need of training. Not only must they be trained in system-specific matters, but also training is often extended into line-specific matters. This is necessary for them to be able to understand the various options offered by an ERP package.

Last but not least, extensive project management skills are needed to work efficiently and effectively toward project goals.

8.1.1 Training of users

The users have to be trained in SAP-specific functions just before project start, otherwise they will forget what they have learned because the line business always takes precedence. Just before project start they appreciate the necessity of learning about the new system.

Implementation of a new system improves processes and procedures, and the users need to be trained accordingly. It is not sufficient to train them in the new system functions alone. The necessary theoretical background must also be provided for them to fully comprehend those new processes and procedures. This business education may take place one or two months before implementation, and should help to make the users aware of what to expect.

The training must be accompanied with documentation of SAP functions, processes, and procedures as a reference guide. The documentation has to be set up by the project team.

After introduction, the users' learning status must be constantly checked. For slow learners or people who joined the company after the introduction, extra training sessions must be organized.

8.1.2 Training of steering committee members

Special attention must be given to training members of the steering committee. These generally are not familiar with the detail of company processes, but they do have a good strategic understanding of how they work in the global context. It is advantageous to exploit their understanding on the one hand, while training them on the other. This can be achieved by thoroughly analyzing the to-be concept for each project.

By presenting the to-be concept in the steering committee, the members get a good insight into future processes, and can judge the concept from their integrated point of view. The to-be concept may be presented by the project leader and supported by the external consultant to provide the committee with the most comprehensive knowledge available. A side-effect of the discussion in the steering committee is that they begin to identify with the new processes and assume ownership of the concept.

Members of the steering committee are not necessarily required to understand the system functions or the screen layout in detail, but they should at least be aware of the basic processes in the system.

8.1.3 Training of project members

Our principle was to grant the project members any training request, as we are convinced that good training is essential for a successful project. This attitude toward training certainly helped us to build up a significant expertise with SAP throughout the company.

System-specific training

The project members should be trained on time: that means not too long before they need the skills, otherwise most of the knowledge is forgotten when it comes to applying it. It even helps to allow people to play with the system first and train them afterwards. The more they know about the system in advance, the more effective the training.

Once the project members are trained, the SAP system has to be installed, otherwise they have no chance to practice what they have learned. With in-house training this can be avoided (see Section 8.1.4).

Information should be given in small doses. People cannot digest all the information given over a two-day course. How can they be expected to remember all the information from the courses if these continue over a period of several weeks?

Line-specific training

We found that project members, and project leaders in particular, not only needed to acquire expertise in SAP but also needed to update their line skills. With the introduction of new software there is also the chance to introduce new business processes (e.g. a new controlling system, new production process, or sales structures). To understand these, and to be able to train the users, the project members need to have a good level of education. It will be necessary to refresh their line know-how with appropriate business courses or specific literature.

Project-management-specific training

The project leaders frequently failed to do their homework regarding the management of their projects. In most cases the reason was a lack of know-how and information. They just did not know how to do their homework. No good results can be expected as long as the project members are not trained well in this discipline. The training may be obtained through a course or by the project manager.

Without doubt, the coaching of project members, particularly project leaders, is one of the most challenging tasks for the project manager. The project manager is responsible for training them in project management work. They must be trained up to the level where the projects become self-supporting units. The project manager acts as coach and consultant for these projects.

8.1.4   Internal versus external training

At the beginning we sent our project members to all the module-relevant courses offered by SAP. We realized very quickly that we needed to revise our training strategy because only about 20% of the knowledge communicated by these courses was relevant to our company's specific needs. The only people who could use all of the information covered in the SAP courses were the project leaders. They require broader knowledge and greater awareness of all the possibilities within their module.

Another advantage of external courses is the contact with SAP and other companies. Yet, in the final analysis, our business processes were too different from those of other companies to allow very close collaboration anyway.

A better alternative to the courses offered by SAP was in-house training by the consulting companies we were using. These courses had the following advantages:

- The consulting company was familiar with the processes and procedures of our company.
- Instruction was given using our own system, data, and customizing. In this way we could test the company processes on the system.
- The training was very efficient because only company-relevant information was communicated, and these courses took about half of the time needed for an SAP course.
- The learning rate of participants was much greater because more individual attention could be given in the smaller groups.
- In most cases the in-house courses proved to be less expensive than their SAP equivalents.

8.1.5   Lessons learned for training

1. **Just-in-time training**   The project members and the users should be trained just in time: that means when they need the skills. If the information is given too far in advance, its relevance is not fully appreciated, and most of it is forgotten when it comes to applying it.
2. **Level-appropriate training**   Every level in the project hierarchy and the various users require different training. The steering committee members need to obtain a good project overview and a general idea of the system's functionality. The project members, particularly the project leaders, must acquire an in-depth understanding of the system's functionality and of project management. The users need to learn those system functions that relate to their jobs, and in addition they must acquire sufficient theoretical background to be able to understand the new processes and procedures.
3. **Have the SAP system installed before starting the training**   Having already been introduced to the system before starting their training, the project members are in a position to get the maximum benefit from the courses. After training, they can immediately put into practice what they have learned.
4. **Train the appropriate people in project-management-specific and line-specific matters**   The project management and the

project leaders need a broader training than the rest of the project members. Above all, they require sufficient project management know-how in order to succeed in the project. Furthermore they frequently need line-specific training for understanding the various processes offered by the system.

5. **Organize in-house training sessions** These are very efficient and comprehensive because they focus exclusively on company-relevant information, and are carried out on the company-specific customized system.

8.2   Project control

As project control is a key aspect of project management, this must be tight. Deviations from the project schedule and the defined project goals must be quickly identified and carefully measured. Progress must be constantly tracked and measured in regular meetings and weekly reports. Such monitoring must be followed up by corrective action where appropriate.

The frequency of the meetings has a direct impact on the success of the project: the more frequently meetings are held, the more efficient and effective the project control, the better the quality, and the faster the throughput time.

8.2.1   Project–controlling cycle

In our experience, overall project control is a continuous cycle. We divided the cycle into four phases: defining, measuring, correcting, and coaching (see Figure 8.1). Starting with the definition of the objectives, the project runs cyclically through all phases of controlling. The controlling wheel keeps on turning until the project goal is reached.

If people lack the know-how to carry out parts of the project, the cycle can also be started at the coaching phase and then proceed to project definition.

The controlling phases are described below.

Defining

To be able to measure a project, objectives have to be defined. We defined overall project objectives in Section 4.1.2. The detailed objectives for each project were defined in the to-be concept (see Section 4.6.2) and in the implementation schedule (see Section 4.5). The objectives mentioned in the to-be concept serve as a guideline for the project. The implementation schedule details the objectives in each project. It describes the different activities and milestones to be reached, and provides detailed feedback on progress at every phase of the project.

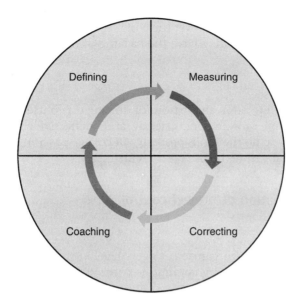

Figure 8.1   Project-controlling cycle.

Measuring

The project must be observed and measured continuously over its whole lifetime. Various controlling tools, such as the implementation schedule, meetings, and reporting, are described.

There are many items to be measured, such as:

- project progress
- implementation schedule: performance against baselines and milestones
- availability of human resources
- time spent
- bottlenecks
- priorities set by the project leaders.

The following items cannot be measured, but have to be observed, because they have a tremendous impact if they are not properly regulated:

- motivation
- communication
- conflicts.

Correcting

The correction of an unfavorable trend is a difficult task. Frequently, people must be remotivated to stay on track. Sometimes a serious talk with the appropriate people involved helps. In other cases, prompt intervention, whoever is involved and whatever the cost, can set things right. Corrections are most effective when they have the backing of the steering committee.

Coaching

We found that quite often the reason for drifting off course was inadequate skills. People were working inefficiently and ineffectively. Coaching can show them how to do their jobs properly. Of course, coaching can also serve as a preventive measure, before tasks are defined.

8.2.2   Organization of project control

Internal control

Project control must be organized at every level of the project organization (see Figure 8.2). The steering committee controls the project manager, the project manager the project leaders, and the project leaders the project team. We found that control was even more effective when it was not only top-down but also bottom-up. The bottom-up approach is an advantage in situations when the level above is acting too slowly or does not realize the problems in a project. That means that the project team itself checks on progress and points out to the project leader or manager the things to consider.

External control

To ensure objectivity, the project should be controlled by external consultants. At the project team level, the projects should be followed by an external module consultant. That person's main concern is the quality of

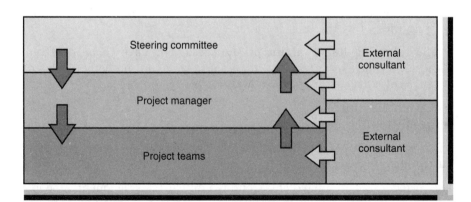

Figure 8.2   Organization of project control.

customizing and the correct setup of the implementation schedule. With the appropriate experience, a good consultant usually has a good insight into the project, and can advise the project team and manager on progress and specific problems.

Another external consultant is needed at the steering committee level. That individual's primary responsibility is to provide consultancy for the steering committee on matters concerning the organization, processes, and procedures. An additional role is to coach and supervise the project manager in the general aspects of project management.

Issue list

As project control is one of the project manager's fundamental tasks, a simple spreadsheet indicating all issues with the appropriate deadlines for every project is an invaluable tool. This is the issue list (see Table 8.1).

8.2.3 Monitoring

Progress is controlled during the whole project. The most important tools are the implementation schedule, meetings, and reports.

Table 8.1 Issue list

Area	Task	Res.	Deadline	Old	Finished	Resource
CO	CO to-be situation revised	HD	25.05.99	14.05.99	24.05.99	
SD	Set up authorizations for claim handling	BE	24.05.99		24.05.99	PT 17.4
CO	Send implementation schedule	HD	25.05.99		24.05.99	Progress meeting
PP-NL	Report list and implementation schedule to send over	KVB	23.05.99		24.05.99	Meeting Sekal
PM	Send implementation schedule	RBR	24.05.99		24.05.99	Meeting Sekal
PP-UK	Update implementation schedule PP SUK	RK	24.05.99	03.05.99	24.05.99	Meeting NW 24.04.99
PM	Training and testing system	RTT	24.05.99		24.05.99	PT 17.4
PT	Check possibility to shut down system of afternoon of 7.6	KVB	31.05.99		28.05.99	PT 14.5
IT	Check exact deadline for transaction for the stock list	EL	28.05.99		28.05.99	IT 23.5
IT	Check PC offer	PBL	29.05.99		29.05.99	IT 23.5
IT	Distribute circular regarding passwords	PBL	29.05.99		29.05.99	IT 23.5

Implementation schedule

The implementation schedule is one of the most significant progress-controlling tools for the project team as well as for the project manager. It is the script for the whole project (see Section 4.5). The schedule must be comprehensive, with no tasks omitted. If important tasks are overlooked, even the best progress control becomes worthless.

The implementation schedule has to be updated regularly to provide a good overview of the project progress.

The project leaders have to send periodic updates of the implementation schedule to the project manager, as this is the main controlling instrument for the project.

Meetings

Progress control is a significant item on the agenda of steering committee and project team meetings where the steering committee members and project leaders officially report on progress.

Progress meetings can also be held in one-to-one talks between the project manager and project leaders or project management members. In such meetings, progress is measured against the implementation schedule and discussed, along with related issues. These more personal meetings often reveal details that would not be raised in the larger, project management team or steering committee meetings.

Meetings should be held regularly and at least on a fortnightly basis, regardless of travel distances.

Here are a few hints for organizing progress meetings at any given plant:

- A visiting schedule sent out a few days before the serves as a useful reminder to all concerned.
- The availability of the project members has to be checked and arranged in advance of the visit to the plant.
- As a courtesy, the organizational head (in our case, the plant manager) should be warned about the visit.
- A meeting with the head of organization (for example, with the plant manager) provides a valuable opportunity to talk about project progress or problems and to solicit help.

Reporting

The weekly reporting (see Section 4.4.1) and the progress meetings serve to keep a close track on progress. The project manager and the project leader have to insist on regular reporting. They must scrutinize the weekly reports for potential bottlenecks (see Appendix, Figures A.3 and A.4) to detect any bottlenecks. On the basis of the reports, corrective action may be required.

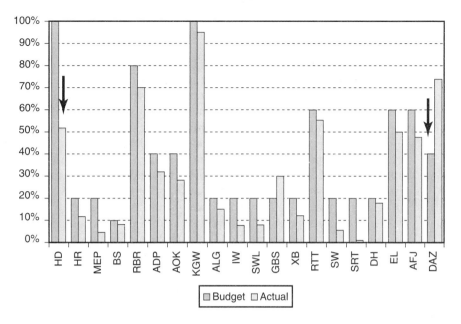

Figure 8.3   Time control.

8.2.4 Time control

The participation of human resources is controlled by weekly reports (see Section 4.4.1). All hours are recorded on a time sheet. As time spent is an early indicator of problems in a project, it is reviewed at every meeting of the project team or steering committee (see Figure 8.3). It clearly highlights problem areas, and indicates where people are spending too little or too much time. In many cases the agreed time distribution percentage was not followed. The steering committee had to take action to bring people back on track, as described in 'Provision of human resources' in Section 4.3.1. In other cases, too much time was allocated: consequently, it had to be adjusted to the actual time required.

8.2.5 Lessons learned for project control

1. **Maintain tight control**   Deviations from the project implementation schedule and from defined project goals must be identified and regularly monitored. Tight control is necessary in order to act immediately on problems or bottlenecks.
2. **Follow the project controlling cycle**   There is a continuous cycle that consists of defining objectives, measuring them, taking corrective action, and giving feedback to project members through

coaching. The controlling wheel keeps on turning until the project goal is reached.

3. **Control the project at every level from every angle** Project control must be organized at every level of the project organization. Internally, the project is best controlled with a top-down and bottom-up approach. External consultants must also control the project at all levels to guarantee maximum knowledge transfer and the highest standards of performance and quality.

4. **Use the implementation schedule, meetings, and reporting to track progress** Progress must be constantly monitored by regular meetings and weekly reports. The frequency of the meetings has a direct impact on the effectiveness of control: the more frequently meetings are held, the more efficiently the project is controlled, the higher the quality, and the faster the throughput time.

5. **Measure and control time-spending** Time-spending in a project is an excellent progress controlling tool. It is an early indicator for problems. If less time is spent than originally agreed, either that task is easy and should be speeded up, or project members are neglecting it, in which case problems will soon emerge.

8.3   Risk management

A risk analysis was set up at the project start to identify, analyze, and respond to risks at an early stage, before they threatened the project. A potential risk that is identified too late may become a real problem, with the following consequences:

- longer throughput time
- additional resources needed (cost and human resources)
- poor quality
- reduced functionality
- project failure (in the worst case).

Risk management certainly cannot solve all problems, but at least it offers a mechanism for identifying and responding to potential threats before the project runs into serious trouble.

8.3.1   Risk identification

Risk management is not just an issue for the project management. Throughout the project, every project member has to be aware of the potential threats and to identify them as soon as possible. In our weekly reporting form (see Appendix, Figures A.2 and A.3) we had a special section called 'Outstanding issues'. The purpose of this section was to get people to

Table 8.2 Project risk analysis

Risk factor	Probability change	Probability before (after)	Measures	Impact before (after)
1. People resign	→	Medium (Medium)	Salary, incentives Backups Motivation Job satisfaction	High (High)
2. Unavailability of people	↑	Medium (High)	Steering committee to provide human resources Delay project	High (High)
3. Insufficient knowledge and training	↓	Medium (Low)	Documentation Training internal/ external Backups Consulting	High (High)
4. Bad external consulting	→	Medium (Medium)	Replace consultant Build up internal know-how Knowledge transfer Documentation	High (High)
5. User acceptance	↓	Medium (Low)	Information, PR and marketing User training Support Individual menus	Medium (Medium)
6. Projects not on time	↑	Medium (High)	Add resources Skip certain functionality	Medium (High)
7. Missing SAP functionality	↑	Low (Medium)	Consulting Step-by-step implementation	High (High)
8. Over-budget	↓	Low (Low)	Set up budget with reserves Correct budget	High (Low)
9. Internal disputes	↓	Low (Low)	Communication Information Steering committee action	High (Medium)
10. Hardware failure	→	Low (Low)	Back up infrastructure Contingency plan	High (High)
11. Software failure	→	Low (Low)	SAP on-line help Software backups	High (High)
12. Lack of information	↑	Low (Medium)	Project bulletin Meeting minutes Communication	Low (Medium)

think about potential risks, and to warn the project leader or the project manager respectively at an early stage. The periodical project team and progress meetings also contributed to risk identification.

8.3.2   Risk analysis

In Table 8.2 we tried to identify and analyze the risks for our project. The columns have the following meanings:

1. **Risk factor**   Circumstances that represent the risk.
2. **Probability change**   Shows how the degree of risk has fluctuated from the original calculation at project start (arrowheads → = no change in probability of risk; ↑ = probability increased; ↓ = probability decreased).
3. **Probability before (after)**   Refers to high–medium–low probability during the project. The values in brackets represent our assessment after completing the project. Such a judgment, of course, depends strongly on the company.
4. **Measures**   Lists the options available for neutralizing the risk.
5. **Impact before (after)**   Categorizes the potential impact; again the values in brackets reflect our judgment after completing the project.

For reasons of simplicity, the probability and the impact of risk occurrence have been rated with the same terminology:

- **Low**   Below 30%, meaning that the risk occurrence may have some influence or a moderate impact on the project.
- **Medium**   Below 60%, meaning that the risk occurrence will have a considerable effect on the project.
- **High**   Higher than 60%, meaning that this risk factor almost certainly will have a crucial impact on the project.

8.3.3   Risk response

Based on the risk analysis in Table 8.2, we took various preventive measures to reduce the probability of risk occurrence:

- **Project member support**   We took good care of our project members. With a good project atmosphere, incentives, special treatment, personal talks, etc., we kept their motivation high.
- **Temporary backup**   Project members with a dual (project and line) function were in many cases allocated temporary personnel to assist them with their line work.
- **Well-trained project members**   We trained and prepared project members well. Any request for specific SAP training was granted.
- **Good consultants**   We were continuously scouring the market for good consultants, and were never satisfied with mediocre consultancy.

- **User information** User acceptance improved after an intensive publicity campaign about the project. We published a monthly project bulletin. Furthermore every opportunity (meetings, functions, etc.) was taken to communicate with the prospective users.
- **Periodic meetings and reporting** We managed risk continuously with periodic meetings and by weekly reporting to detect problems early.
- **Software know-how** Regarding missing SAP functionality, we had to rely fully on our consultants. This is one of the reasons for getting the consultants to participate in formulating the to-be concept. They could advise us at that stage about the software's functionality.
- **Sufficient financial resources** A comprehensive budget was set up, and included sufficient contingency to support unexpected costs during the project.
- **Avoidance of internal disputes** We pursued a good communication and information strategy to prevent internal disputes. Furthermore we set up a strong project organization with the full commitment and ownership of the steering committee and a strong project management.
- **Secure hardware and suppliers** With a hardware contingency plan, reliable hardware and suppliers, we secured our hardware infrastructure perfectly, preventing bottlenecks.

8.3.4 Reflection on risk analysis

After the project implementation we reflected on our risk analysis (Table 8.2). We tried to find out whether our risk assessment during the project was correct. We recorded our experience as below, and reviewed the accuracy of our assessment regarding the probability and impact of risk occurrence.

- **Resignations** Three of our project members resigned after the project because we could not offer them an appropriate job (see Section 8.3.5). Nobody resigned during the project, however. While the project lasted, the project members were motivated and satisfied with their job because it was a real challenge for them. In addition we paid good incentives and in certain cases increased the salary. *Medium* was the correct probability of occurrence for this risk factor.

    A resignation during the project definitely would have had a *high* impact on the project, and probably would have delayed the project; it could not have been compensated by a backup but only by a consultant.
- **Unavailability of people** In many cases the agreed time percentage for project work was not followed. This was especially the case with part-time members of the project team. The steering committee had to

take action to get people back on track. The impact on the project depended on the project member's function. Mostly the full-time project members had a *high* impact, while the insufficient participation of others had *medium* or *low* impact.

The probability of risk occurrence was correct for the full-time project members, but for the part-timers it was more accurately described as *high*.

- **Insufficient knowledge and training** Insufficient knowledge and training can indeed endanger the project, because incorrect customizing can have a disastrous effect on the project. We experienced this in one of our first projects. The impact was *high*, because the module did not work properly. If the training is done as described in Section 8.1 and an external consultant looks after the project, the probability of risk occurrence is then *low*.

- **Unsatisfactory external consulting** As long as there is a deficiency of experienced SAP consultants on the market, the risk of getting poor consulting still occurs quite often. Therefore the probability of risk occurrence can be defined as *medium*. It cannot be rated as *low* because finding a really good consultant is still quite difficult.

  The impact remains at *high* because inadequate consulting can lead to incorrect customizing and, ultimately, to system problems.

- **User acceptance** We discovered that the probability of risk occurrence for acceptance of the system was *low* and not *medium* as originally estimated. Ownership by top management, open information, and good training helped to bring down the probability of risk occurrence from *medium* to *low*.

  The impact is still categorized as *medium* or even *low*, since once an enterprise software package has been implemented, there is very little chance to go back to another system. The user might as well accept the system. On the other hand non-acceptance by the user often reflects mistakes made during the implementation: for example, bad information and communication policy, user not involved early enough, or insufficient training.

- **Projects not on time** Tight project progress control is necessary to keep projects on track. The probability of risk occurrence has to be changed to *high* because the timing is always a critical and crucial point in a project. In our experience, the impact also must be set at *high* because delays involve substantial extra resources.

- **Missing SAP functionality** In most projects we had problems reflecting certain processes and procedures in the standard software. The search for new solutions was very difficult and time consuming, even for consultants. Based on this experience, we would set the probability of risk occurrence to *medium* and leave the impact as *high*.

- **Over-budget** Our budget was well estimated, and therefore the probability of risk occurrence was *low*. The impact of spending more money than budgeted was overestimated. When taken in the context of company profits, an over-spend here would not seriously endanger the company, and so the impact could be set at *low*.

- **Internal disputes** The atmosphere on the project was good, and therefore the probability of risk occurrence was correctly estimated. If there were personal differences, the team was able to overcome them. In the event of political struggles, we estimated the impact as *medium* because the individuals concerned could be replaced.
- **Hardware failure** We had about two software failures within these three years. Thus the *low* risk status we gave to this factor was accurate. The impact certainly was *high*, because the whole company could not work with the system.
- **Software failure** We had about two software failures within these three years. Thus the *low* risk status we gave to this factor was accurate. The impact certainly was *high*, because the whole company could not work with the system.
- **Lack of information** We realized that a good information policy helps the project implementation tremendously. The risk level has to be set at *medium* because this factor is often neglected. The impact is at least *medium*. The better people are prepared for a project, the less resistance is built up among the users.

8.3.5 Risk of resignation

We have included this section on the resignation of project members, because we believe that this is an important topic for risk management.

Three of our project members resigned after the project because we could not offer them an appropriate job. Fortunately they resigned after and not during the project, but the loss of expertise is still unfortunate. All three of them joined consulting companies.

People need a vision during and, very importantly, a challenge after the project. During the project it is easy to motivate project members with that vision. Clear objectives, tasks, and responsibilities help the project members to identify themselves with the project.

After the project some people go back to their line job; others have difficulties with returning to it. A project is comparable to an intensive education for the participants. Certain people improve their expertise and potential tremendously. These people also need a challenge and a clear vision beyond the project. The most convenient solution is to show people their future prospects before the project gets under way, and this will also serve to keep them motivated and enthusiastic during it.

It is for the project manager to raise this issue at steering committee level. The committee should then discuss every project member's future and take whatever action may be appropriate.

The risk of resignation can be minimized by the following measures:

- **New job**   The best solution for these project members is a challenging job that suits their newly acquired skills. Although these people are not in the project environment any longer, at least their know-how is still available to the company.
- **Increase salary**   For people with SAP skills their market value increases considerably, as they are in great demand on the market. They should be paid a salary in line with the going rate, or at least given a generous bonus in recognition of their extra contribution to the company. However, increasing their salary risks disrupting the whole salary structure, and if they return to their former line jobs, it may cause difficulties.

We also had negative experiences with using employees who were not well rooted within the organization. Such people have no clear vision before they start working in the project. During the project they behave quite well since they acquire a vision and become rooted in the project itself. They are able to increase their market value considerably with their SAP involvement. SAP experience will enhance their market value and career prospects, and they will exploit this to find another job once the project has finished.

Whatever the case, it is advisable to have a good backup for every key project member.

8.3.6   Lessons learned for risk management

1. **Identify, analyze, and respond to a risk**   Appropriate risk management can prevent a longer project throughput time, the need for additional resources, poor quality, reduced functionality or, ultimately, the failure of the whole project. Discussing risk management makes people aware of the threats to be expected during a project.
2. **Reduce the probability of risk occurrence**   Throughout the project, every project member has to be aware of the potential, and must help to identify them as soon as possible. Meetings and reports play an important role in this respect. To be able to take preventive measures and to reduce the probability of risk occurrence, a risk analysis should be organized at the beginning of the project.
3. **Secure the hardware infrastructure**   The hardware has to be well secured, as the company depends strongly on the availability of the IT infrastructure. With a hardware contingency plan, reliable hardware, and a dependable supplier, we perfectly secured our hardware, preventing technical bottlenecks.

4. **Reduce the risk of resignation** The project members are the most valuable assets in a project. Therefore they need to be well looked after. A good project atmosphere, incentives, special treatment, intensive communication, human resources support, etc. keep the project members' motivation high, and avoid the risk of resignation.

8.4 Change management

8.4.1 Preparation for change

The implementation of an integrated standard software package such as SAP has a major impact on a company and especially on its employees. The usual reaction to major change is resistance. Resistance is a natural and inevitable reaction to a disruption of expectations. We understood that resistance to positive change is just as common as resistance to negatively perceived change, and both reactions follow their own respective cycles, which have to be anticipated and managed (see Figures 8.4 and 8.5).

We prepared our staff for the coming changes in the following ways:

- **Through management support** Once the management had assumed ownership of the project, it set an example for the whole company and supported the project throughout the organization.
- **Through information** Publishing a monthly project bulletin (see 'Project bulletin' in Section 4.4.4) kept the company informed about the project. Project presentations at important meetings were also used to keep everyone informed about developments.
- **Through communication** Informal contacts with users were also explored at an early stage of the project. Users could express their concerns and fears frankly and openly in one-to-one talks.
- **Through training** Good training is essential to prepare the people for the new system. They have to get acquainted with the various functions of the new system, and acquire confidence in operating it.

8.4.2 Change perceived as negative

A minority of our users perceived the IT implementation as negative. The 20–80% rule can also be used here. About 20% of our users were negative toward a new system, and extremely difficult to deal with; 80% were in favor of the system. The people with a negative attitude followed the typical cycle shown in Figure 8.4.

- **Shock** They were shocked when looking at this new system for the first time. Everything seemed to be so complicated, user-unfriendly, and not at all like the old system they were used to and could operate well.
- **Disbelief** Based on these fears, they perceived the change as very negative, and could not really believe that this system could help them in their daily work.
- **Anger** The frustration turned to anger once they realized that they would have to work with this system.
- **Negotiation** After realizing that the project was fully supported by our top management, and that there was no way out, people started to ask for help and support in their daily work. The project team tried to make access to the system easier by installing user-specific menus.
- **Depression** The negotiation phase could not make the system any easier for them to handle. This confrontation with reality gave way to a depression phase.
- **Understanding** Only after going through the depression phase were they really ready to learn and understand the system.
- **Acceptance** Finally, even these people accepted the new SAP system, but it needed a lot of effort and strength from the project team to guide them through the various phases.

Those people who perceived the change as negative wanted to hold on to the old system. They wanted no change. In fact, we discovered the following reasons for this:

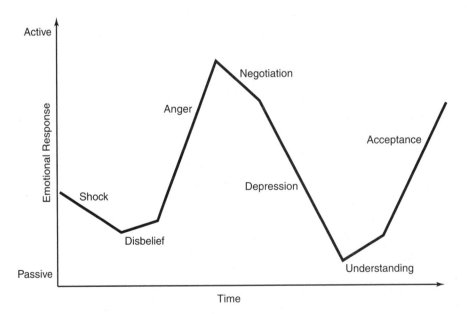

Figure 8.4 Change perceived as negative.

- They were afraid of losing ownership of their data.
- They were afraid of failure.
- They envisaged a substantial loss of social contacts.
- They were too lazy to respond to change.
- They were afraid of structural changes.
- They had other difficult personal or business concerns.

8.4.3   Change perceived as positive

Most people were looking forward to getting a new system. They perceived the change as positive, and went through the cycle shown in Figure 8.5.

- **Uninformed optimism**   These people had a basically positive attitude toward the expected implementation without knowing exactly what to expect, but were optimistic about getting a good working tool.
- **Informed pessimism**   They became doubtful after first contact with the system, because it is not easy to get to know an integrated software package such as SAP.
- **Checking out**   They started to compare their experience with that of a previous system changeover or with system implementations they had heard about publicly or from friends.
- **Hopeful realism**   With their feedback from other similar situations in private or public and their positive attitude toward the implementation, they appreciated the extent of change for operating such an integrated system.

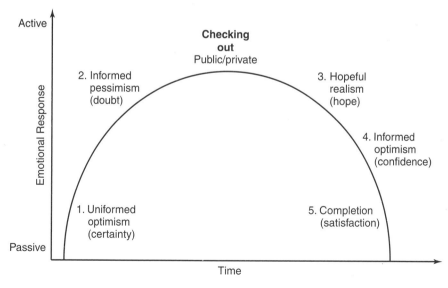

Figure 8.5   Change perceived as positive.

- **Informed optimism** They learned fast, and gained confidence in operating the system.
- **Completion** Knowing the system well, they were able to retrieve the necessary information fast and efficiently, and appreciated having a tool that really helped to make their lives easier.

People were generally satisfied with the system because they recognized the following opportunities:

- The wider use of data throughout the company and the access to data from different individuals and departments increases the individual employee's insight into company-wide processes and procedures.
- The implementation of an advanced information system makes contact with colleagues easier and more efficient than before.
- A more advanced system gives individuals the possibility to grow in their jobs. They become more adaptable, and can branch out in their work.
- Fast access to customer data empowers them in their dealings with customers.

8.4.4 Coping with change

About 80% of the people assimilated well to the new system because they had the necessary energy to cope with an IT change. According to Figure 8.6, an

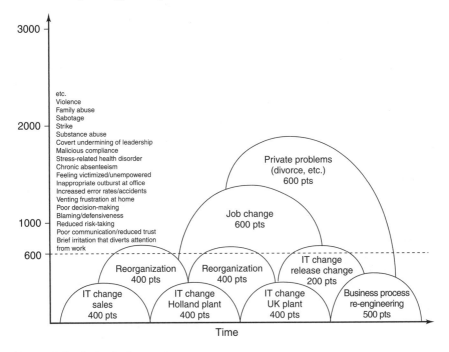

Figure 8.6 Assimilation points.

average person can deal with changes below 600 assimilation points, for example with an IT change, a reorganization, or a business process re-engineering exercise. Assimilation points are a measurement of the energy used to assimilate change. When a person must deal with a situation exceeding 600 points there is the probability of change-related dysfunction. Significant changes in life, such as divorce or cumulative change, can overwhelm an individual's capacity to assimilate the new situation: 600 points are exceeded. An IT change combined with a reorganization, for example, may cause change-related dysfunction. Change-related dysfunction starts with irritability and the tendency to be easily distracted, continues with poor communication and lack of trust, through chronic absenteeism, and ends finally with strike, sabotage, or even physical violence.

That is one of the reasons why we tried not to combine our IT change with business process re-engineering. In a few cases we had to adjust or reorganize processes, and this in itself caused some dysfunction for some people. We found change-related dysfunction especially in those departments where we combined the IT change with other projects.

Among the 20% of the employees who had problems adapting to this major change, we observed the following symptoms:

- **Poor communication** As they distrusted the system these people shunned help, not even asking for advice when they had serious problems.
- **Increased margin of error** As a result of their difficulties with handling the system, their errors increased.
- **Shifting responsibility** The system was blamed for all kinds of problems and errors.
- **Stress-related health disorder** Overwhelmed by the changes at work, many people, especially those in management positions, were extremely stressed when the new system was introduced. In a few cases this led to serious illness.

Those people who had a negative perception of the changes received the following support:

- **Communication** We approached these employees from various sides to encourage them to discuss their problems.
- **Education and training** We specifically targeted them for education and training to help them overcome their problems.
- **Information** We identified and explained difficult processes and procedures in our project bulletin (see 'Project bulletin' in Section 4.4.4). E-mail was used for communicating and explaining system-specific problems and changes.
- **Job transfers** In several cases we transferred people to other positions within the company.

- **Replacement** In a few cases the introduction of the IT system had such an impact on the job that it was more than they could handle and we had to replace them.

8.4.5 Conclusion

A common reason for dysfunction was the fact that people were incapable of adapting to the increased demands of the job resulting from the system change. In certain jobs the system required different or additional skills, which some people were incapable of acquiring.

Approximately 15% of people at the plants had extreme difficulties in handling the system correctly, and needed extensive support. Some of them even had to be replaced. However, such people had probably reached their limits before the implementation of the IT system. Frankly, the new system just highlighted weaknesses already existing within the organization.

In Sales Administration about 40% of the staff had severe difficulties with operating the system. These people needed, and still do, a lot of support from our hotline. Intensive training brought their skills up to a level where they could carry out the basic functions required by their job.

The organization as a whole comes under pressure during an implementation of an integrated system. All the additional projects, the as-is and to-be concepts, etc., expose all the pre-existing weaknesses within the various departments.

Line managers were in a particularly stressful situation, with dual roles in project and in line work. This demands vast reserves of energy and skill in order to be effective. In this way management's strengths and weaknesses were also revealed, and quite a few were unequal to the task.

8.4.6 Lessons learned for change management

1. **Manage the change** Project members, especially those on the steering committee and in project management, should be aware of the changes they are initiating with the project. They must manage the changes actively, and help the users to make a smooth transition. This means guiding them, communicating the information, and providing them with education and training throughout the respective project cycles.

2. **Focus specifically on persons who perceive the change as negative** Such people are usually a minority, but they need the most attention. They are probably not the most adaptable employees or the easiest to deal with, but for that reason they will require special coaching from project members.

3. **Do not accumulate changes**   The implementation of integrated standard software demands a great deal of energy from the users. Too many simultaneous changes should be avoided, because they may overstretch many individuals' capabilities and result in change-related dysfunction.

4. **Expect about 20% of users to have serious difficulty**   Such people cannot cope with the changes and the increased demands of the job. They require extensive support, and some of them may even need to be replaced.

5. **Reorganize only where necessary**   Changes always reveal the underlying strengths and weaknesses of any organization. As a result, some reorganization may be unavoidable so as to have the right people on the right job.

6. **Consider changes carefully but implement them resolutely**   With the introduction of a new system, job transfers or redundancies are unavoidable. Structural changes must be thoroughly evaluated. However, once a decision has been made it must be carried out quickly and with determination: the longer action is delayed, the more difficult it will become.

9 Closing phase

With all of its objectives achieved, the project enters its final stages. In our case this involved:

- Analyzing and documenting project results.
- Formally handing over the project to the line organization.
- Reintegrating project members into the line organization.

Such project-closing activities should not be left until project completion. It is advisable to initiate the closing phase straight after implementation. This will ensure that no significant or useful information is lost; that the line organization realizes its responsibility for the product; and that the future deployment of project members can be properly discussed. After implementation it is also important to maintain the project's momentum, because pressure from the steering committee will slacken off, and the programme could go into rapid and premature decline.

9.1 Project analysis and documentation

Project analysis and documentation involves collating project records, ensuring that they reflect project objectives, analyzing success and effectiveness, and archiving all of this information for future reference.

We documented our project from the very beginning. This was the basis for the extensive analysis and the material presented in this book. It enabled us to measure project performance and draw lessons for future projects. The documentation itself represents a valuable source of corporate information.

9.2 Handing over the product to the line organization

The product of the project must be handed over to and accepted by the line organization. A successor organization also needs to be established, its tasks and responsibilities defined, and its administration set up.

9.2.1 SAP coordination organization

Organizational structure

After implementation, the project organization remains active until all problems are solved and the necessary follow-up projects are implemented. Once this is done, the product should be handed over as soon as possible to the line organization, which then assumes ownership of it. The project organization is then converted into an SAP maintenance and coordination organization, which is line oriented, and responsible for the stabilization, maintenance, and improvement of the SAP system.

This conversion is necessary on the following grounds:

- **Objectives** These have now changed, and are better reflected in the new SAP coordination organization.
- **Ownership** The line organization must take over full responsibility for and ownership of the implemented system.
- **Management** Whereas project management demanded a radical strategy, SAP coordination needs a consolidating approach.
- **New blood** People eventually tire of project work, and at this point it is a good policy to provide extra human resources, wherever possible.

The structure of the new organization is illustrated in Figure 9.1.

It is structured as a matrix organization: vertically, the SAP coordinators are responsible for all SAP matters at any given site; horizontally, the module coordinators represent their respective modules. On the one hand, this structure ensures flexibility to solve SAP-related problems quickly and effectively at any site; on the other hand, it guarantees uniformity within each module.

Functions in the SAP coordination organization

- Management team:
  - The steering committee was dissolved. On specific SAP issues, the SAP coordination team was to report directly to top management, who could then discuss them in their own meetings, as necessary. Since many top managers had also been on the steering committee, the actual change was barely noticeable.
- SAP coordination team:
  - The project manager was replaced by the SAP coordination manager. Managers highly experienced in SAP are best suited to the new position, although it is not full-time.
  - The project management team was replaced by the SAP coordination team. Most of the SAP coordinators were former project management members. SAP coordinators had to devote between 20% and 40% of their working time to SAP matters at each site. The exact time

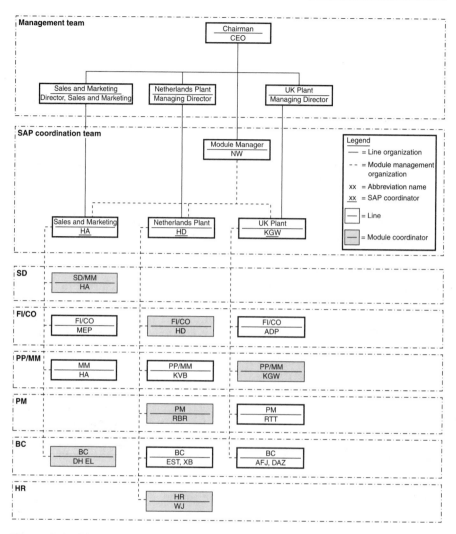

Figure 9.1 SAP coordination organization.

commitment depended on the modules they were responsible for and the workload from running projects. We appointed a representative for Sales, the Netherlands plant, the UK plant and one for IT. Since the organization is more line oriented, an IT representative should also be included in the module team to coordinate IT matters with line demands. In our case, the SAP coordination manager also represented IT, and so a special appointment was unnecessary.

- Module coordinators and module leader:
  - Module coordinators have to ensure uniformity within their modules. In our case, mostly the SAP coordinators filled this role.

- The module leader is in charge of maintaining and improving the live SAP application. This task should require only a modest investment of time, and the role was mostly undertaken by key users from the line organization.
- The IT department was no longer centrally available for all projects. Instead, IT was integrated locally at each site.

9.2.2   Tasks and responsibilities

Tasks and responsibilities of the SAP coordination manager

The SAP coordination manager has the overall responsibility for the SAP modules. His particular duties are:

- to manage the SAP coordination
- to coach the SAP coordinators
- to detect and solve problems and conflicts
- to conduct public relations
- to communicate and report to top management
- to provide quality assurance.

Tasks and responsibilities of the SAP coordinator

- To coordinate SAP matters at a site
- to represent the site on the SAP coordination team
- to continuously improve SAP functions and procedures
- to research the latest developments in SAP
- to educate and train the module leader
- to communicate with and report to the SAP coordination manager and the line manager.

Tasks and responsibilities of the module coordinator

- To coordinate SAP matters within a module
- to maintain the SAP modules
- to continuously improve SAP functions and procedures
- to research the latest developments in SAP
- to educate and train the module leader
- to communicate with and report to the SAP coordination manager.

Tasks and responsibilities of module leader

- To oversee a specific module
- to evaluate change requests and discuss them with the line manager, and with the SAP and module coordinators
- to solve functional and technical SAP problems

- to configure and customize the system
- to evaluate new SAP functionality and make proposals for change
- to test and implement new releases
- to train and support users
- to communicate with and report to the module coordinator
- to create and maintain the module-specific documentation.

9.2.3 Administration of the SAP coordination organization

Reporting

After handover, reporting is no longer necessary for the newly implemented projects, but it must be maintained for the follow-up and action-list projects.

Once the transition from the project organization to the SAP coordination organization had been made, weekly reporting was focused on the running projects. This ensured at least a minimal feedback from these projects.

Meeting pattern

SAP coordination team meetings must take place on a regular basis. We opted to hold these meetings every four months. The remit was as follows:

- to coordinate activities
- to report on progress
- to provide a rapid response to problems
- to exchange information.

SAP coordinators also hold regular SAP meetings with the SAP leader at each site.

9.3 Reintegration of project members

The reintegration of project members into the line organization is a sensitive issue. Most committed project members undergo extensive personal and professional development in the course of the project. They acquire knowledge of project management, learn about the company's processes and procedures, become experts in their module area, and increase their specific line skills. As a result, they gain in confidence and potential. When they return to their former line positions they are ready for fresh challenges, and may even demand them.

Some of our project members became dissatisfied with their former line jobs, and were looking for more stimulating challenges elsewhere in the company. Such people, project leaders in particular, suffered an identity crisis as the end of the project approached, since the company had not clearly defined their future role in the organization. Their subsequent appointment as SAP coordinators did not entirely overcome their alienation because, however interesting, it still remained essentially a part-time role. This presents a dilemma for the company, as an appropriate new job is not always available and yet the company would not want to lose such highly trained employees. Therefore it is essential that these people discuss and agree upon their career development with their line managers before the project ends. The whole issue should be brought to the attention of the steering committee early enough for them to take the appropriate measures.

9.4   Lessons learned from the closing phase

1. **Document the project**   This material will enable an in-depth analysis to be made of the outcome. Project performance can be measured and lessons drawn for future projects. The documentation itself constitutes a valuable source of corporate information.

2. **Set up a maintenance and coordination organization**   An integrated standard software package also needs maintenance after its implementation, and therefore an appropriate organization with clear tasks and responsibilities must be established. The conversion of the project organization into a maintenance organization, the reporting, and the meeting structures should be prepared during the closing phase.

3. **Initiate the reintegration of project members early**   The reintegration of project members into the line organization must be considered well in advance by the steering committee. Subsequently, it will be difficult to find a suitable role for project members, with their newly acquired skills and abilities. Nevertheless, they must be presented with fresh challenges if the company is not to lose them.

10 Special problems during project implementation

10.1 Material master maintenance

Our company produces foam, which is delivered in rolls. As we are totally customer oriented, we deliver any roll length and width our customers require. However, we were soon faced with the problem that our SAP system was unable to handle the different roll lengths for the same product. That forced us to create a material master for every product with a different length and width. We add about five new materials each day and, consequently, our material master has tripled within the last three years.

While our material master was rapidly expanding, we also found that maintaining it within SAP was awkward and time consuming. Additional human resources were needed, and we appointed one extra person for the Netherlands plant and one in Sales. In the UK plant material master maintenance required a half-time employee.

The main complaints from the management side were:

- That it took about 15 minutes to enter a new product from start to finish in the PP module, and about 20 minutes in the SD area.
- That a low-level, low-cost employee would be unable to maintain the bill of material, the routings, and the work centers, and that a highly skilled individual who knows company processes and procedures must be appointed to the task.
- That many calculations were not offered automatically by the system, and some that were made in SAP were inaccurate, especially where specific entry fields do not allow decimal figures. These calculations had to be made outside the system, for example in Microsoft Excel, and then written in. There was a danger that incorrect figures could be entered.

Our solution was the development of our own input screen for the sales and plant areas. The material master input screen combines all relevant input fields on one screen. All necessary calculations are made in the background. The information is transferred via batch input to the original material master screens.

The automation of the material master input saved us one person in Sales, and considerably reduced the amount of work in the plants.

10.2   Data accuracy

Soon after the MM and PP modules went live in the Dutch plant, we discovered a large amount of incorrect data in the stock environment. The reason was inaccurate data input by the warehouse manager. With the introduction of our costing module (CO-PA) we realized that even more data in the system was incorrect. In the material master, above all, we identified inaccuracies in the master data, bills of materials, and routings. Once again, the problem had arisen partly as a result of incorrect master data input by the individuals concerned. However, in this case, the main cause was not that the data had been inaccurately transferred but that the actual source data was incorrect. This inaccuracy had gone unnoticed because the data had not been used for controlling purposes.

We investigated the problem in a follow-up project. To resolve it, we built in various cross-checking programs. These programs check the value of error-prone fields, and print an error log for the attention of the module coordinator.

In addition we issued the following guidelines:

- The line manager is responsible for his processes and the data in those processes. He must implement an effective control mechanism to guarantee data integrity.
- The module coordinator has the duty to cross-check the data in his module and inform the line manager about discrepancies.
- Everyone should be aware that, with an integrated system such as SAP, the effect of wrong data input is not confined to one particular department as before but spreads across the whole company.

The quality of data is not only maintained by the system; it also depends on people.

10.3   Program errors

The most serious problems in our implementation were program or customizing errors, because it was very time consuming and mission critical to solve them. If there were customizing errors it was our problem, and we had to find a solution fast. On one side, we were supported by our consultants and, on the other, by the SAP hot line.

Unfortunately, we encountered several program errors. To trace and replicate each error was very time consuming as it involved lengthy correspondence with SAP. Some problems were solved immediately with the help of consultants from SAP, while others took weeks to sort out.

10.4   Make-to-order or make-to-stock production

One of our most difficult decisions concerned the production method within the SAP PP module. Our SAP standard software offered two alternative production philosophies: make-to-order and make-to-stock. About 30% of our business is make-to-stock and 70% make-to-order production.

How can we define make-to-order and make-to-stock?

- Make-to-order production is a manufacturing process in which a product is normally made once only. Each product is made to the customer's specifications. An order has to be received prior to production. Make-to-order amounts to 70% of our business.
- Make-to-stock production supplies products from stock; it is assumed that the product is already available. The production is planned to maintain stocks and not for a specific customer. Make-to-stock totals about 30% of our business.

Between these two choices, our company faced a dilemma because we are neither an exclusively make-to-order nor make-to-stock company, and yet we had to opt for one or the other of these alternatives.

The advantages and disadvantages are listed in Table 10.1. Essentially the decision is between detailed financial reporting and detailed logistical

Table 10.1 Comparison of make-to-order and make-to-stock

Make-to-order

Advantages	*Disadvantages*
1. Direct link production order/sales order	1. No target costs or variance
2. One text taken over automatically	2. No stock valuation
3. Faster sales order information	3. Two production methods. More administrative work for over-production (stock-to-stock)
4. No batch management needed	4. Move from order related to non-order related stock is a problem
5. Production costs for each sales order	5. Complex for organization: different production methods (sales, costing). No combination of several production orders/products

Make-to-stock

Advantages	*Disadvantages*
1. Target costs and variance available for each product	1. No link to sales order
2. Stock valuation	2. No link to sales text
3. One production method	3. No production costs/sales order item
4. No changes for Sales	4. No distinction in non-order related/order related stock. More administrative work to access information (due to dynamic allocation)
	5. No material requirements planning needed
	6. No reservation of stock for a customer

control. Make-to-stock is preferable for improved financial analysis of production results. Make-to-order, however, is recommended where a direct link is required between a customer order and a production order.

The steering committee decided unanimously in favor of make-to-order. Their rationale was that, since we are a customer-oriented company, our future would be in order-related business. Furthermore the plants are run on the basis of logistical and production performance measurements, rather than by detailed financial analysis. With make-to-stock, the steering committee found pitfalls in the manual links to the sales order, the increased departmental workload, the non-allocation of stock, and the inability to trace sales orders. Taking all of these factors into account, preference was given to logistical control and therefore to the make-to-order process.

10.5   SAP program add-on

10.5.1   Problem description

ALVEO faced the problem that several independent production orders could not be combined in one production run. We decided to program with ABAP tools an add-on to the SAP standard production environment.

We called our development SAP-X. SAP-X saved us a lot of time in daily production by allowing us to combine and control several production orders in one run. The disadvantage, of course, was the high development cost of about SFr40,000 and the maintenance work with every release upgrade.

10.5.2   General description of the add-on program

SAP-X was designed to provide ALVEO users with an additional set of transactions and information to control daily production. The following developments have been realized, and are outlined below:

- The creation of a collective production order (run number).
- Change transaction on the collective order data.
- Confirmation per run number (also called reel or sheet registration).
- Correction of confirmations;
- Various reports.

Creation of a run number

A run is a combination of one or more production orders that have the same production process. The user can enter a work center, planning period range, and the type to be produced. Hence they get an overview of all production orders to be scheduled on this work center.

The production planner selects the orders to be combined in one run and 'posts' the run. SAP-X creates a run number for these production orders and eventually a change in the production order data.

A run has to be created for every single production order. Even if no combination can be made a run number has to be created.

Change transaction

A change transaction has been created to allow the modification of production orders. To alter the table, a reorganization function is available.

Confirmation of a run number

The most important part is the confirmation per run. The production and non-production hours, the setup time and the scrap material must be confirmed.

The confirmation results in a posting, which initiates the following background transactions:

- Confirmation of the hours and quantities for the production order(s).
- Backflushing of the raw materials (the backflushing indicator is set for each raw material).
- A cost center posting for non-production hours.

Various production reports

The following reports are available:

- Shop floor papers: extruder order, weighing/blending paper, foaming order.
- Production reports: daily, weekly, monthly.

The reports are based on the run and/or sheet information, combined with production order and sales order information.

11 Conclusions

11.1 Thirteen factors for a successful implementation

Over the four years we implemented 28 projects, we had the chance to experiment, putting to the test and improving our project management knowledge, tools, and techniques. We achieved many successes but also made many mistakes. The main thing was to learn from the ups and downs of our experience. The many lessons brought together in this book clearly demonstrate that we had a lot to learn, even where we thought we knew everything.

Looking back on our experiences, we drew up the list of key success factors below:

1. **Ownership assumed by the management** Top management must play an active role in the project. They need to participate on the steering committee and take over ownership, to support the project with their expertise, and to endow it with the necessary authority. Active participation by upper management is crucial to the adequate resourcing of the project, to taking fast and effective decisions, and to promoting company-wide acceptance of the project.

   Departmental managers must also be members of the project team to assume project ownership, and to contribute the necessary line know-how. Doing this, they also keep themselves up to date with the system.

   Ownership taken over by the departmental manager is again a clear signal to the department staff to accept the project. At the same time, departmental managers usually know the most about processes and procedures in their departments, and can therefore provide the best support for the project.

2. **Relationship of trust among the project members** Trust among the project members including members of the steering committee is essential for a successful outcome, because the project organization has hardly any hierarchical authority but must rely on natural authority, which involves trust. Without trust an extensive coaching and controlling effort is needed to prevent a rapid decline. Trust can be built up with intensive communication, coaching, delegation of responsibility, personal care and attention, among other things.

3. **Simple, clear and measurable project objectives**   Well-defined object-ives help to keep the project constantly focused, and are essential for analyzing and measuring success. They must clearly defined, measur-able, and controllable, and the savings must be quantified for each objective.

4. **Effective and strong project management**   The project management has to lead, manage, and coach the whole project. To fulfill this task efficiently and effectively, the management needs broad authority over all aspects of the project. Their authority should be sufficient to permit the project management to engage in all necessary managerial and technical actions required to complete the project successfully, regardless of organizational barriers. The more powerful the project management, the better the chances for a successful implementation. If the project management falls below par in its tasks and respons-ibilities the project is likely to fail, since it plays a key role in the whole project.

5. **Clear and simple project organization**   A flat and streamlined organ-izational project structure is very effective, with its short communication and decision lines, especially between the project management and the steering committee. Problems can be tackled quickly and unbureau-cratically. Clearly defined tasks and responsibilities at all levels of the project organization allow everyone to work efficiently toward project goals, avoiding political struggles over matters of authority and control.

6. **Highly qualified project members**   Project work is very demanding and complex, and therefore requires people with a high learning potential. The project will need capable members from the line organization. High-calibre project members ensure a fast and proper implementation. As the driving force of the whole project, members of the project management team must be particularly skilled and able. Any project organization is only as good as the individuals that it comprises.

7. **Full-time project members**   Adequate human resourcing is essential. At the very least, all key project members must be available full-time to ensure project continuity and progress. If human resourcing is inadequate, the project is likely to make only slow progress, and ultimately may disintegrate. Part-time project members always tend to give higher priority to line work, since it is easier and more convenient for them to do.

8. **Open and honest information policy**   Open and honest communica-tion is of paramount importance to satisfy the information needs of users, and to prevent the circulation of unfounded rumors. Users need reliable information, because any project affects them directly and may even threaten their jobs. The open information policy helps the user to become acquainted with the new situation, to build up confidence in the project and its members, and finally to accept the project.

9. **Conversions and interfaces ready on time**   The conversion and interfaces must be ready in good time to allow for the data transfer and data verification. The amount of time needed for planning, programming, converting, and testing the data is often underestimated. Missing or incorrect data will delay or may even jeopardize the project. It is important that the conversion and interface issue is addressed during the planning phase, and that it is programmed and tested in the realization phase. Conversion is not just an IT matter, completed with the technical data transfer. The data should be checked and tested after conversion by the project members and key users before it is released into production.

10. **To-be concept as project guideline**   The to-be concept is the foundation and guideline for the whole project. All relevant matters concerning the future organization, processes, procedures, and methods must be thoroughly researched, discussed in depth, and recorded in writing before commencing the realization phase. A comprehensive and well-set-up to-be concept protects the project team from lengthy disputes about the customizing of the module, and therefore avoids any delays from the line side.

11. **Good consultants improve throughput time and quality**   A great deal of know-how is essential for the complex implementation of an integrated standard software package. The success of a project depends strongly on the capabilities of the consultants because the consultant is the only one with in-depth knowledge of the software. Hence good consultants have a major impact on the throughput time and the quality of a project.

    An external consultant on the project team must help with customizing, setting up the implementation schedule, and controlling the project. A consultant at the steering committee level is needed to advise it about organization, processes, and procedures, and to assist the project manager.

12. **Business process re-engineering after project implementation**   Business process re-engineering should be carried out after, and not before or during, the project implementation. Doing the business process re-engineering before the SAP project would be inadvisable because the functionality and therefore the real potential of the software is not fully known at that time. Furthermore, political disputes arising out of business process re-engineering may disable the whole project or at least create very unfavorable conditions for the forthcoming SAP project. Business process re-engineering undertaken during the SAP implementation is likely to fail, because if these run concurrently, most employees will not manage to assimilate or adjust to all the changes.

13. **Regular and continuous project control**   The project should be tightly controlled, as this is the essence of good project management.

Any deviation from the implementation schedule and defined project goals must be identified and tracked carefully, with appropriate corrective action taken. Progress must be measured constantly and reported regularly in weekly meetings. The frequency of the meetings has a direct impact on the effectiveness of control: the more frequently meetings are held, the more efficient and effective the control, the better the quality, and the faster the throughput time.

11.2   Project analysis

After completion, it is vital to analyze and measure the success of the project. Success has been achieved insofar as savings and benefits for the company can be proven.

We considered the following aspects of the project:

- objectives (see Section 11.2.1)
- strategy (see Section 11.2.2)
- cost (see Section 11.2.3)
- throughput time (see Section 11.2.4)
- non-financial benefits (see Section 11.3).

11.2.1   Project objectives analysis

Objectives and savings per module

Referring to the objectives set at the beginning of the project (see Table 4.2), we analyzed our savings and report the results in Table 11.1. Savings are indicated only for those objectives where we really could prove a direct and unequivocal link to the project implementation.

Conclusion on project objectives

The project objectives were clearly formulated and the savings indicated. For the most part the objectives were reached, although not all of the estimated savings were actually made. The shortfall arose mainly out of unrealized savings in operation ratio and yield. Although the objectives were well founded, too little research was available in regard to the impact of an IT system implementation. Operation ratio and yield cannot be improved by an SAP implementation. There are other factors such as technical equipment and personnel that have a higher impact on improvement of operation ratio and yield.

SAP does not necessarily produce savings in human resources. In our experience, such savings are possible where repetitive processes are automated and personnel savings on this level can be obtained. However, at the

Table 11.1 Project objectives analysis

Objective	Expected savings (SFr)	Actual savings (SFr)	OK
1. To ensure that response time on inquiries will be below 2 hours		Customer satisfaction	✓
2. To ensure reliability of customer response			✓
Result Both goals were reached with the integrated on-line system. Sales, production or finance data can be obtained instantly, and the customer information is based on real data. The attainment of these goals cannot be measured in financial terms, but they certainly help to satisfy customer needs.			
3. To optimize sales administration	100,000	250,000	✓
Result Many processes in the sales area were streamlined and automated. This enabled ALVEO, on the one hand, to save on three people in the administration, and, on the other hand, to expand without the need for extra sales office staff. Since ALVEO's sales managers can access adequate and reliable data, and the management can track progress better, fewer meetings are necessary, and a lot of traveling expenses are saved. ALVEO estimates these savings at a minimum of SFr250,000 p.a.			
4. To improve the balance between customer requirements and material availability		Customer satisfaction	✓
Result Customer order information and the stock overview were clearer and more easily controlled. The company was able to set up a more efficient master production schedule and so improve the balance between customer requirements and material availability.			
5. To reduce average payment terms by 5 days	80,000	100,000	✓
Result SAP advanced controlling tools managed to reduce outstanding payments from 75 to 70 days. This saves ALVEO some SFr100,000 p.a.			
6. To optimize routine financial administration		150,000	✓
Result Although ALVEO's turnover had doubled over recent years, no additional personnel were required in finance. This was possible thanks to SAP's automated processes and procedures. Information is faster and more easily accessible, which again saves money on meetings and traveling costs. ALVEO estimates the savings at around SFr150,000.			

Table 11.1 (cont.)

Objective	Expected savings (SFr)	Actual savings (SFr)	OK
7. To reduce throughput time (order planning and production) by 50%, from 8 to 4 weeks		Customer satisfaction	✓
8. To reduce stock by 40%	580,000	300,000	–
9. To double stock turnover	370,000	370,000	✓
10. To improve the operation ratio by 1%	600,000		–
11. To improve yield by 0.5%	300,000	Customer satisfaction	–

Result The throughput time was improved by at least 50%, in some areas by even more. The improvement was possible through a combination of various measures. Some of these were SAP related: the software enabled ALVEO to gain a better, more comprehensive overview of the planning and production processes. Along with SAP, ALVEO also introduced a new foam-planning method. Some projects not directly related to SAP also helped to improve the throughput time, but even these were indirectly related in that they arose out of the SAP implementation.

This is another goal where it is difficult to put a precise figure on savings. The savings were certainly substantial but, more significantly, achieving this goal helped ALVEO to provide a faster service to its customers.

Result A stock reduction of about 60% was made in Sales. In the plant, however, the target reduction was not met, and reached only around 20%.

Result This goal was achieved. Stockholding was reduced from one month to half a month. At a shipment rate of 350 tons per half month, using 10,500 m² per month, using 10,500 m² a day, at a cost of SFr2.5 per m², the total saving comes to SFr370,000 for 2 weeks.

Result For the two goals mentioned above, the introduction of the SAP system was just one among many factors that contributed to the improvement. To make substantial progress in this area all elements of business management (organization, information technology, processes, procedure, and methods) must be brought up to the same level. Improving the IT environment alone has little impact on these goals. Follow-up projects are needed to make progress in the other business areas.

Table 11.1 (*cont.*)

Objective	Expected savings (SFr)	Actual savings (SFr)	OK
12. To increase overall output by 2.5% with the same number of staff	500,000	500,000	–
Result ALVEO has increased its output by considerably more than 2.5% since implementation. As already indicated above, this increase was brought about by various factors, not exclusively related to the SAP implementation. Nevertheless, it may be claimed that an increase of this magnitude would not be achievable without a sophisticated ERP package such as SAP R/3.			
Total annual savings in SFr	2,530,000	1,670,000	

same time, the implementation of a highly complex integrated software package such as SAP demands additional highly qualified people to deal with all the system information and the process control. After the SAP implementation ALVEO established a controlling department to process all the SAP data and prepare it for management.

Another lesson we learned was that, with a long project throughput time of $3\frac{1}{2}$ years, it may be necessary to revise objectives in the light of new knowledge acquired during the implementation.

11.2.2   Project strategy analysis

Experience regarding the strategy

Looking back on the strategy we set at the beginning of the project (see Section 4.1.3), we assessed it in the light of our project experience (see Table 11.2).

Conclusion on project strategy

The chosen project strategy was a good fit for our project. Its clearly defined parameters helped to give the project a common orientation in the right direction. The preference for implementation by our own staff, as expressed in item 4 in Table 11.2, has proven to be an approach with both a positive and a negative side. The advantage is the concentration of know-how within the company. The disadvantage is that that after the project its highly trained members will be looking for comparable challenges, and if they cannot find them within the company the risk is that they will find them elsewhere. In that case, their considerable expertise is lost to the company. For those who transfer to non-SAP functions within the company, they will soon become deskilled as they lose touch with the rapid, ongoing developments in SAP. For these reasons it may be preferable to opt for more external consulting, since external consultants would continue to be available as and when needed, and they would always be up to date with the latest functionality in each module.

11.2.3   Project cost/savings analysis

General explanation of the cost/savings analysis graph

In Figure 11.1 we have analyzed the estimated and actual annual running costs; the estimated and actual annual savings; and the annual savings less accumulated running costs.

The whole project cost over one year is shown in the 'Estimated and actual annual running costs' graph. The investment costs are included in

Table 11.2 Project strategy analysis

Project strategy	OK
1. We intend to implement the SAP R/3 system for all our affiliates in Europe to serve the accounting, controlling, sales, production and logistics functions.	✓
Result We implemented the FI, CO, SD, and MM modules in all our European affiliates. Additionally, we implemented AM, PP, PM, and HR at our plants.	
2. We shall adopt a step-by-step and a roll-out approach, introducing the different modules at each site throughout Europe.	✓
Result The two approaches proved to be right under consideration of the complex implementation environment, the limited resources, and the available functionality.	
3. Deadlines established in the implementation schedules are to be met at all costs.	✓
Result All modules have been implemented in time except the CO-PA, module which was rescheduled by 3 months, because of technical problems. The other modules have been introduced in time or even before deadline (see Section 11.2.4).	
4. The project is to be implemented by our own staff. Consultancy should be kept to a minimum and project members trained up as appropriate.	✓
Result Our project members were so well trained that they could even do the consulting themselves for the project roll-out at the UK plant.	
5. Major focus is to be put on management support at all levels.	✓
Result After we adjusted our project organization (see Section 4.2) we received the necessary support by the management.	
6. We plan to implement the SAP R/3 software without modifications to its source. We shall adapt and standardize our organization, processes, and procedures in accordance with the standard software SAP R/3. Any change to the SAP R/3 software will require approval by the steering committee.	✓
Result Only after receiving correction notes from SAP, did we modify the source. Our SAP-X extension (see Section 10.5) is an add-on program, and involved no modifications of the source.	
7. We propose the use of a central computer based in Switzerland, with the plants and sales offices being connected via wide area network (WAN).	✓
Result The concept of using a central computer and a WAN proved highly successful, and response times were good across Europe.	

the running costs in the form of depreciation. Internal costs for human resourcing are not included.

The annual savings achieved through the implementation of the SAP R/3 package are represented in the 'Estimated and actual annual savings' graph. This is based on the savings indicated for each of the project objectives (see Section 11.2.1). Savings after 1998 are estimated.

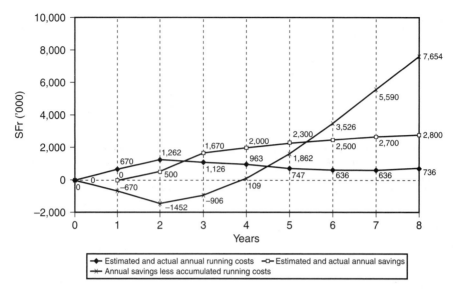

Figure 11.1 Cost/savings analysis.

The 'Annual savings less accumulated running costs' graph is an aggregate of all running costs with the annual savings compared so as to determine the time taken to reach breakeven point.

All graphs are explained in detail in the sections below.

Estimated and actual annual running costs

- **Year 1** Our annual running costs totalled SFr670,000 to start up our project phase with the SD, MM, and FI modules.
- **Year 2** Costs peaked at SFr1,282,000. Extensive consulting was required because many projects went live in the second year (see Table 2.1). In addition, for the first time, full maintenance costs for SAP, HP, and our wide area network had to be paid.
- **Year 3** Running costs fell back slightly to SFr1,126,000 since we were able to cut down on consulting costs with internal consulting.
- **Year 4** Costs fell in all areas because all modules in all sites were implemented except the HR module and the follow-up projects.
- **Year 5** The projects were finished. Hardware and software, hardware extension, and depreciation costs were ongoing.
- **Year 6** The costs of hardware and software purchased at the beginning of the project are written off.
- **Year 7** A gradual increase of the annual running costs in subsequent years is expected as hardware upgrades arising from release upgrades take place.

Estimated and actual annual savings

- **Year 1**   No savings were made as the project was not in production yet.
- **Year 2**   After introduction of the FI, SD, and MM modules, substantial savings were realized. According to Table 11.1 we achieved cost savings of SFr500,000 in these modules.
- **Year 3**   In the third year we implemented the CO and PP modules. We made savings of SFr300,000 by stock reduction and SFr370,000 on faster stock turnover. The overall output had increased by over 2.5%, which resulted in savings of at least SFr500,000. This adds up to savings of SFr1.17 million. Together with the previous year's savings the total reached SFr1.67 million.
- **Year 4**   All the SAP modules were implemented. The follow-up projects and business process re-engineering projects started will produce their initial results in forthcoming years. Approximate savings of about SFr350,000 may be expected.
- **Year 5**   Owing to the process re-engineering projects, the estimated savings will increase year on year, since non-IT changes arising out of the SAP implementation will then take effect. We expect annual savings of well over SFr2 million.

Annual savings less accumulated running costs

- **Year 1**   As no savings were possible during the first year, our annual running costs totalled SFr670,000.
- **Year 2**   During this period our accumulated project costs amounted to SFr1.45 million. After our first implementations, savings became substantial and started to bring down the overall project cost.
- **Year 3**   At the end of our project period, running costs dropped and savings rose, which initiated a steady decline of the accumulated project costs.
- **Year 4**   Less than 4 years after project start, the project breakeven point was reached.

Conclusion on project cost

Until the third year, annual savings of SFr1.67 million could be realized. The project reached the breakeven point less than 4 years after project start. From the fourth year onwards continuous savings of over SFr2 million a year will be possible.

The calculation takes no account of capital cost and internal costs. If an internal cost of about SFr2 million were factored in, the breakeven point would be reached 5 years after project implementation.

11.2.4   Project throughput time analysis

Within our program we implemented 28 SAP modules within the period of 3 years (these are listed in Figure 11.2). The total program can be divided roughly into three implementations over this period, following a step-by-step and roll-out approach (see Section 2.2.4). We managed to implement 8 projects before deadline, and 19 on time with one delayed.

Deadline principles

Meeting deadlines was our number one priority for every project. Delay had to be avoided at all costs. We were prepared, if necessary, to invest in additional consulting or temporary human resources. Our justification was on the grounds of:

1. **Cost**   Any project delay costs the company additional money. We calculated the weekly cost for a project delay as SFr40,000 internal and SFr40,000 external costs.
2. **Human resources**   If human resources are tied up with the project longer than scheduled, of course, they will be unavailable for other projects or for line work.
3. **Trust**   Every time a project is delayed, confidence in it is shaken. The project then risks going into terminal decline.
4. **Motivation**   Any delay depresses morale. Project members may easily become disheartened by missed deadlines and the resultant lengthening of the project.

Project implemented after deadline

The profit analysis project (CO-PA) suffered a two-month delay for several reasons:

- **Program error**   The search for a solution to a program bug in the CO-PA area added approximately 2 months onto the implementation schedule.
- **Extension of project scope**   The scope of the project was widened to include a new task, the sales order settlement, which originally was not part of the CO-PA project. Implementation of the CO-PA project had revealed the gap that normally would have been dealt with by the logistics group.
- **Human resources**   Too little time had been devoted to the project.

Based on the calculation of SFr80,000 for a week's delay, the one delayed project out of the 28 incurred about SFr2,850 costs per week. Hence the delay of the CO-PA project cost us about SFr22,800.

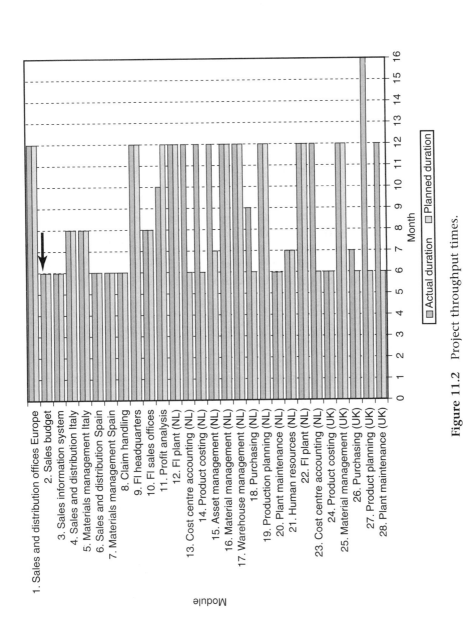

Figure 11.2 Project throughput times.

Projects implemented before deadline

We managed to implement eight projects before the deadline for the following reasons:

- **Increased SAP and project management know-how** The more projects we implemented with our step-by-step approach, the better our SAP expertise and project management skills became. When experienced project members were assigned to new projects, they increased the efficiency and effectiveness of those projects.
- **Internal consulting** As described in Section 4.3.2, our own experienced people provided consultancy for the roll-out at the UK plant. They possessed the unique combination of familiarity with the company's processes and procedures together with SAP-customizing expertise. They knew better than any external consultant the special customizing features needed by the firm, and were therefore able to speed up the implementation considerably.
- **Good external consulting** In some projects we had very efficient and goal-oriented external consultants, who also helped to accelerate the implementation.
- **Few technical problems** In these projects we were confronted with relatively few technical problems. Those program errors that did occur were easily corrected within a short time.
- **No changes of project scope** The teams implemented their projects in close accordance with the to-be concept. Since the concept had been discussed in depth, no extension of scope and no additional requirements needed to be considered.

The eight projects implemented before deadline altogether saved us 43 months of project work. Calculating the weekly cost for a project delay as savings, theoretically we saved about SFr490,000.

Conclusion on project throughput time

We implemented almost all the projects within or before the given timeframe. The fast throughput time saved us about SFr465,000 of project cost. Accelerated throughput times not only reduced costs but also kept motivation high.

We opted for a step-by-step implementation because we wanted to reduce complexity, had limited resources available, and were keen on building up our own knowledge base (see Section 2.2.1). A throughput time of $3\frac{1}{2}$ years is still a long time for a company the size of ALVEO, even for a program consisting of three implementations. The project demanded a great deal of dedication from all of its members as well as substantial guidance from the steering committee and the project management team. The conflict between a fast throughput on the one hand and reduced complexity, limited resources, and a good internal knowledge base on the other must be solved by every company individually, as few are completely identical in their structure, resources, management, etc. We would maintain that our approach was the right one considering ALVEO's internationalization, its resources, its structure, and, last but not least, the multi-site implementation.

11.3 Non-financial benefits

Our SAP project had a great impact on the ALVEO company. Not only did the project save ALVEO costs, as described in the previous section, it also benefited the company in other areas, which cannot be expressed in financial terms, but still have a considerable benefit for the whole company. These intangible benefits can be described as follows:

1. **Customer satisfaction** ALVEO is now in a position to serve the customer better and faster with on-line information, for example about the status of a particular order.
2. **Control** The integrated software allows the ALVEO management to receive the necessary data for leading and controlling all business processes of the company.
3. **Efficiency and effectiveness** The arrival of the SAP system introduced new processes and procedures into the company, and confronted the organization with detailed information about itself. This information, along with the new possibilities, forced ALVEO to re-think and re-engineer its business processes and procedures. The re-engineered processes definitely helped it to increase efficiency and effectiveness.
4. **Flexibility** Changes are necessary to keep a company agile. The IT environment had been completely transformed, but ALVEO still needed to bring its processes, organization, procedures, and methods up to the same level as IT. Such a task requires a great deal of organizational flexibility.
5. **Speed** The re-engineering of the logistics and production processes helped ALVEO to decrease throughput time by 50%. Furthermore, instant on-line access to customer order information allowed a faster response to customer enquires.
6. **Mutual understanding** An integrated system integrates the company. All processes within a company have to be coordinated among the various departments. Departments are forced to cooperate with each other and work closely together because they must share the same basic data. People come to realize their strong interdependence. To build up an integrated system it is necessary for people to communicate with

those involved in the processes preceding and subsequent to their own. In this way everyone learns about the whole process chain, and gets a better perspective on other people's problems. The SAP project substantially improved mutual understanding at all company levels and in all functions of the company.

7. **Information**   A huge information potential was created by linking all business applications together into one integrated system. ALVEO now gets on-line information and high-quality data.

8. **Education**   By participating in the project, people were educated in project work, which was very valuable for the company. Furthermore, staff in all areas (finance, logistics, production, and sales) had to boost their knowledge considerably to handle the new processes, procedures, and methods offered by the system.

9. **Structures**   Software processes and procedures are designed to be clear and straightforward. Implementing the software without modifications, the company had to restructure itself to conform with the processes prescribed by the software.

10. **Time**   As all information is centrally available, many progress meetings could be eliminated. In the remaining meetings, time was saved because discussions were better focused as the accuracy of the figures was no longer in question. All information was received faster.

11. **Quality**   The SAP software helped to improve the company's quality standard because all the business organization, processes, procedures, and methods had to be reviewed, adjusted where needed, and documented in detail.

11.4   Overall conclusion

Many of our project goals were accomplished. Considerable savings were made. Most projects were implemented on time, and a few ahead of schedule, with just one delayed.

With the introduction of SAP, ALVEO now saves an annual SFr2 million. Besides the financial savings, ALVEO has also benefited in other areas such as customer satisfaction, efficiency, flexibility, speed, and mutual understanding. In addition, the project exposed organizational, procedural, and process-related weaknesses within the company, and enabled their correction through the various process re-engineering projects.

Consequently, our SAP R/3 can be declared a success. Our success came not because there were no problems, but rather because those problems were successfully overcome. That is how we met our project objectives.

Dr Jean-Pierre Sormani, CEO of ALVEO and Chairman of the FuturA steering committee, summed it up as follows:

'We are sure that the SAP implementation helped to increase the company's efficiency and effectiveness. With the implementation of the integrated standard software package SAP, we have laid a solid foundation for future growth. It gives us a competitive advantage, helps us to reduce costs, to be more flexible and faster in the market and, most important of all, to serve our customers better.'

Appendix:
Documents

Figure A.1   Detailed project organization   156

Figure A.2   Project leader's report form   157

Figure A.3   Project members' report form   158

Figure A.4   Report summary   159

Figure A.5   Meeting agenda   160

Figure A.6   Progress reporting   162

Figure A.7   Minutes, project management team handling   163

Figure A.8   FuturA Bulletin   164

Figure A.9   Detailed implementation schedule   166

Figure A.10 Authorization request form   172

Figure A.11 Test procedure for migration   174

Figure A.12 Time schedule for migration   176

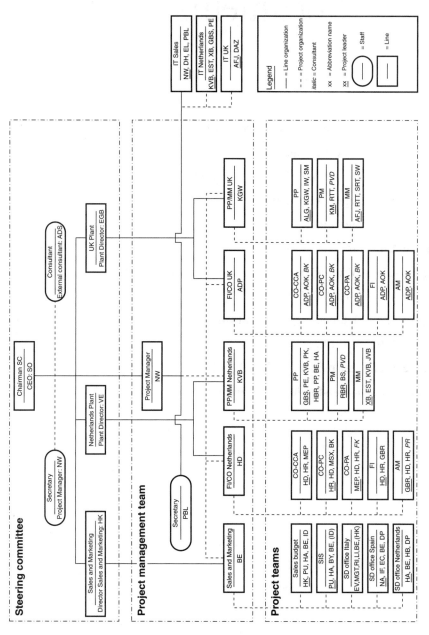

Figure A.1 Detailed project organization.

FUTURA PROJECT REPORT WEEK: 37 Date: 8 September 1998 **8004**

Module/Location: Production UK	Subproject: Production planning	In time:	Yes ☑	No ☐

Outstanding issues:

Integration meeting has been organized

AL on holiday next week

	Initials	KGW		01 Traveling costs
	Costs in SFr	300		02 Training costs
	Expenses code	03		03 Other expenses

ID	**Performed activities:**	KG	AL	SW	IW
	Preparation for conversion	24		10	
	Making user manual	8			
	PP/FI discussion	2	2	2	2
	Miscellaneous	3			
	Total time	**37**	**2**	**12**	**2**

ID	**Activites next week:**	KG	AL	SW	IW
	Continuing with conversion preparations	20		12	
	User manual	8			

Figure A.2 Project leader's report form.

PROJECT REPORT WEEK: 35   **Date:** 30 August 1998

Module: BC	Subproject: EL	In time: Yes ☑ No ☐

Performed activities (planning)	Mo	Tu	We	Th	Fr
BC administration (tape-drive problem, evaluation)	1	3	2	3	2
SD ZSBIC009 batch Input (change for BE)			2		
SD ABAP ZSORC009 (claim handling) change for HA	2	1			
SD language problem customer master sales text					
SD New ABAP for text determination ZSZZC001				2	4
FI problem for MEP (OSS inquiry)				1	
SD problems (OSS: wrong language, not possible to post goods issue for delivery)	2			2	
Total time	**5**	**4**	**4**	**8**	**6**

Costs in SFr			
Expenses code			

Codes for expenses:
01 Traveling costs
02 Training costs
03 Other expenses

Activities next period	Mo	Tu	We	Th	Fr
Merthyr visit	X	X	X	X	X
SD ABAP master sheet					
Total time					

Outstanding issues

–Input for ABAP master sheet still incomplete

Figure A.3 Project members' report form.

PROJECT report wk 35

	Outstanding Issues		
EL Merthyr stay 2–27 September 98			

Subprojects	Performed activities week 35	Activities week 36	In time
FI/CO-PA	Discuss human resources and availability Study implementation plan	Check on document release change Define start to-be concept, set deadlines/items	Y
PM SKL	Present to-be situation in SC meeting	Presentation to the department Module organization structure	Y
FI/CO SUK	To-be situation. Invoice verification PP/CO discussions with KGW Solve problems re outside lamination	Meet Sekal Set up test data Solve/identify problems UK – calculations	Y
PP/MM SUK	Prepare for conversion User manual PP/FI discussions	Continue with conversion preparations User manual	Y
PM SUK	Notifications Start setup of no. 5 extruder worksheet in line with SAP coding system Discuss PM module with EGB	Set up worksheet for no. 5 extruder in line with SAP codes	Y
MM-PUR SUK	Work on to-be situation Customizing	Working on to-be situation Customizing	Y
BC	BC administration ABAP programming Problem solving	ABAP programming and solving problems	Y

Figure A.4 Report summary.

Time frame

Time	Subject	Responsible
0830–0845	1. Project organization	NW
0845–1115	2. Progress reporting	BE, HD, KVB, ADP, KGW
1115–1130	3. Cost/time spending	NW
1130–1215	4. Project specific topics	KVB, KGW, HD
1215–1300	Lunch	
1300–1430	4. Project specific topics	KVB, KGW, HD
1430–1545	5. Miscellaneous and reserve	NW

1. Project organization

1.1 Minutes last PT meeting	NW
1.2 Project implementation schedule	NW

2. Progress reporting

2.1 Sales and distribution

2.1.1 Claim handling	BE
2.1.2 Authorizations	BE

2.2 Finance Sekal

2.2.1 CO-PC	HD
2.2.2 CO-CCA	HD
2.2.3 FI	HD

2.3 Production Sekal

2.3.1 PP	KVB
2.3.2 MM	KVB
2.3.3 PM	KVB

2.4 Finance Sekiuk

2.4.1 CO-PC	ADP
2.4.2 CO-CCA	ADP
2.4.3 FI	ADP

2.5 Production Sekiuk

2.5.1 PP	KGW
2.5.2 PM	KGW

Figure A.5   Meeting agenda.

3. Cost/time spending

3.1 Project costs	NW
3.2 Project time spending	NW

4. Project-specific topics

4.1 SAPX	KVB
4.2 As-is situation PM Sekiuk	KGW
4.3 Revised to-be situation CO-PC	HD
Demo order flow	KVB/HD
Top critical points of the month	NW

5. Miscellaneous

5.1 Release change (testing procedure)	NW
5.2 Client copy	NW
5.3 Opening hours of production system	NW
5.4 HP machine	NW
5.5 Archiving of data	NW
5.6 SAP-Comdes conversion after PP implementation at SKL	KGW

Date PT meetings

Date next PT meeting: 14 May 98 Merthyr

Figure A.5   Meeting agenda (*cont.*).

Progress reporting

Project: PP	Location: NL
Meeting: Project Team Meeting	Date: 22.10.98

Milestones	Start date	Finish date	% complete
Planning phase	1.3.98	31.5.98	100
Realization phase	1.6.98	30.9.98	95
Preparation phase	1.10.98	31.12.98	65
Production phase	4.1.99		

Actual status:

Data installed
Converted data checked
Movement types/postings checked
System check
Basic training completed
SAP-X tested

Future activities:

Determine authorizations
Draw up training plan
Define final conversion requirements
Conduct training sessions
Carry out implementation

Outstanding issues:

Data conversion

Figure A.6   Progress reporting.

FUTURA	Project management	Date: 9 Aug 98	Page 1 of 1
ALVEO AG	Bahnhofstrasse 7, PO Box 2068, CH-6002 Lucerne/Switzerland Tel. (041) 228 92 92		Fax (041 228 92 00)

TO:	KVB, HD, ADP, KGW
CC:	SO, HK, VE, EGB, NY, BE, BO, SMS, WSP, HR, MEP, MSX, GBS, CONSULTANTS: SLI Franz Köpper (FK), Arno de Schepper
FROM:	NW/PBL
DATE:	
SUBJECT:	PMT-MEETING DATE:
LOCATION:	MERTHYR

MINUTES:

MOST IMPORTANT POINTS:

4.1 Project experience: pros and cons
4.2 Follow-up projects are listed in Appendix 1
5.3 A new client copy will be carried out at the weekend

TO DO LIST:

Subject	Resp.	Due Date
Required human resources from SKL to be defined	KGW	
Customizing of planning structure	HR	
Conversions to be specified with EST	KGW	

FuturA organization

Minutes last PMT meeting

The minutes from the last meeting have been approved.

Detailed implementation schedule

After the advancing of the MM-PUR SUK and invoice verification SUK, the following projects are left for the following period: assets management SUK (AM), human resources (HR), quality management (QM), follow-up projects according to Appendix 1.

Progress reporting

Production Sekal

Plant Maintenance

					1998				1999				
Task name	**Start**	**Finish**	**Base Start**	**Base Finish**	Qtr 4	Qtr 1	Qtr 2	Qtr 3	Qtr 4	Qtr 1	Qtr 2	Qtr 3	Qtr 4	Qtr 1
PM SKL	01.04.98	01.01.99	01.01.98	01.04.99										
Planning phase	01.04.98	29.08.98	01.04.98	19.08.98			86%							
Realization phase	01.07.98	01.01.99	05.08.98	15.11.98				0%						
Preparation phase	02.12.98	01.01.99	09.09.98	31.12.98					0%					
Production phase	01.01.99	01.01.99	01.01.99	01.01.99						01.01				

Actual status:
Finalize to-be situation
Involve key users in auditing

Future activities:
Presentation to-be situation in SC
Check to-be situation with other modules
Prepare realization phase

Figure A.7   Minutes, project management team handling.

FUTUR**A** BULLETIN

MERTHYR ON BOARD

This year, Sekiuk will be fully involved in our SAP projects. By the end of the year, the

Production Planning, Controlling and Plant Maintenance modules will be introduced. For all areas we have a representative in the Project Team. George Williams (KGW) is responsible for the production and logistics modules and Andrew Purchase (ADP) for the finance modules. Elton Bridges (EGB) represents the SAP projects on the Steering Committee.

All project members are highly motivated and looking forward to the implementation of SAP at their plant.

We wish them all the best for their projects.

Norbert Welti

DO WE NEED A SYSTEM LIKE SAP?
Interview with Prof. Dr. Arno de Schepper

What is your role in the implementation of FuturA?

I see three aspects.

Firstly, my relationship with top management. As an independent advisor, with lots of experience in implementing complex systems, I can counsel top management on what they have should do for the project, and eventually also on what must change in their own way of doing things, and that, of course, is easier for an outsider than for an ALVEO employee. Secondly, I provide assistance to the project manager on aspects of project management and project control.

Thirdly, where needed, I give input on the ways of working in logistics and its relation with Marketing/Sales and Production.

Why does ALVEO need an independent advisor?

For a start: the FuturA project is big, complicated and costly. The value of an independent advisor is, if you select a good one, that he has gathered experience in other companies. He can transfer part of the learning curve from other situations to ALVEO.

What is important on FuturA for the management of the business?

It is important to understand what FuturA is. This diagram may help:

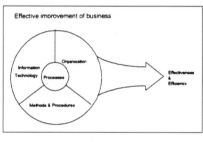

To improve effectiveness and efficiency of business management you have to improve and to bring into proper balance with each other four basic elements: the processes, (simple, straightforward, reliable); the organisation (distribution of tasks and responsibilities and adequate people); methods and procedures (adapted to the product/market combinations); and the information (the system and the measurements). FuturA is not only a SAP information system, it also has repercussions on the ways of working and the organisation.

FuturA improves coordination between all company levels and functions. The most important quality of FuturA is that the experience of commercial, technical and accounting departments is brought together to function as one coherent team.

Continued on page 2

Figure A.8   FuturA Bulletin.

FUTURA NEWS

We congratulate Xavier in de Braek (XB) on the birth of his son, Kye.

As from 1 March 96 onwards, David Zeraschi (DAZ) is 100 % available for the IT department in Sekiuk.

Marjon Schreurs (MSX) is supporting the CO-PC and FI projects in Sekal for 50%.

A successful ABAP training session was carried out by C'tac for the IT people.

The Release change to 2.2E took place on the test machine. This new Release will be installed on the production machine on 23/24 March 96.

Certain people, especially the young ones, have problems recovering from Carnival. They get sick or have very "erotic" voices ...

By moonshine and snow the PT members enjoyed a relaxing atmosphere in the Swiss mountains. While having an excellent dinner top secrets were revealed. It came out that a Dutch man attended a boys' school when he was young. The relationship with his friends must have been unbelievably close. They even chase him to Switzerland and mention strange room numbers on the phone. Who knows what these numbers mean and what happened in these rooms?

We all know that the Dutch are the best, greatest and most famous people in the world. They discovered America and Siberia, have the biggest balloon, the greatest soccer team etc. etc. etc.

PROFILES

Prof. Dr. Arno de Schepper is professor of Logistics at the University of Brabant in the Netherlands. He is also an independent advisor in Logistics and Business Management. He has a long-term relationship with ALVEO management. It is now twelve years since his first assignment at ALVEO's Roermond factory. This was in the period when he was starting up the consultancy practice for PricewaterhouseCoopers in the Netherlands. He was also a speaker for ALVEO in Luxor.

Arno de Schepper is married, he has five children and is also a dedicated gardener on his farm.

DO WE NEED A SYSTEM LIKE SAP?
Interview with Prof. Dr. Arno de Schepper (from page 1)

This can be observed best in the goods flow in the company as all departments have a great interest in it. The results include among other things: Shorter delivery times; better customer service; reduction of stocks; and better operational performance. These elements should be quantified so that their success can be followed and checked.

What impact will FuturA have on the way we work?

People are normally afraid of losing ownership of data and also will have less social contacts than before the introduction of the system.

It is true that data is no longer owned exclusively by any one individual or small group. But the wider use of data in the company and the access to data of other individuals and departments increases insight into overall company process and brings everything closer to the individual.

Regarding social contacts, the following observations are valid: Social contacts depend, above all, on the individuals themselves. We all know that individuals in the same function and at the same level have very different social behavior. The change to an advanced system makes contacts more efficient but also makes them easier.

More advanced systems give individuals possibilities to grow in their functions. I sincerely hope that many people from the ALVEO group will exploit the increased opportunities created by FuturA.

Arno de Schepper

| Editors: | FuturA Project Management | Coordinator: Petra (PBL) |
| Editorial Address: | ALVEO AG, Bahnhofstrasse 7, 6002 Luzern | |

Figure A.8 FuturA Bulletin (*cont.*).

Task name		Compl (%)	Duration (days)	Start	Finish	Actual finish
1 Planning phase		0	85	04.01.99	30.04.99	NA
1.1	*Project scope*	0	10	04.01.99	15.01.99	NA
1.1.1	Project definition	0	10	04.01.99	15.01.99	NA
1.1.2	Project obectives	0	10	04.01.99	15.01.99	NA
1.1.3	Project strategy	0	10	04.01.99	15.01.99	NA
1.2	*Project organization*	0	10	04.01.99	15.01.99	NA
1.2.1	Organizational structure	0	10	04.01.99	15.01.99	NA
1.2.2	Steering committee	0	10	04.01.99	15.01.99	NA
1.2.3	Project management	0	10	04.01.99	15.01.99	NA
1.2.4	Project team	0	10	04.01.99	15.01.99	NA
1.2.5	Projects	0	10	04.01.99	15.01.99	NA
1.2.6	IT team	0	10	04.01.99	15.01.99	NA
1.2.7	Consulting team	0	10	04.01.99	15.01.99	NA
1.3	*Project resources*	0	10	04.01.99	15.01.99	NA
1.3.1	Human resources	0	10	04.01.99	15.01.99	NA
1.3.2	Consulting	0	10	04.01.99	15.01.99	NA
1.3.3	Cost	0	10	04.01.99	15.01.99	NA
1.4	*Project administration*	0	20	04.01.99	29.01.99	NA
1.4.1	Reporting	0	11	04.01.99	18.01.99	NA
1.4.2	Time recording	0	11	04.01.99	18.01.99	NA
1.4.3	Meeting management techniques	0	11	04.01.99	18.01.99	NA
1.4.4	Information and communication	0	11	04.01.99	18.01.99	NA
1.4.5	Project facilities	0	11	04.01.99	18.01.99	NA
1.4.6	Project standards and procedures	0	11	04.01.99	18.01.99	NA
1.4.7	Project handbook	0	15	11.01.99	29.01.99	NA
1.5	*Project implementation plan*	0	10	18.01.99	29.01.99	NA
1.5.1	Create implementation schedule	0	10	18.01.99	29.01.99	NA
1.5.2	Discuss implementation schedule	0	10	18.01.99	29.01.99	NA
1.5.3	Finalize implementation schedule	0	10	18.01.99	29.01.99	NA

Figure A.9 Detailed implementation schedule.

Task name	Compl (%)	Duration (days)	Start	Finish	Actual finish
1.6 Concepts	0	65	01.02.99	30.04.99	NA
1.6.1 As-is concept	0	20	01.02.99	26.02.99	NA
1.6.2 To-be concept	0	45	01.03.99	30.04.99	NA
1.6.3 Reorganization	0	22	01.04.99	30.04.99	NA
1.6.4 Coordinate activities with other modules/departments	0	22	01.04.99	30.04.99	NA
1.6.5 Set up responsibilities	0	22	01.04.99	30.04.99	NA
1.7 Technical environment	0	35	11.01.99	26.02.99	NA
1.7.1 Define strategy for technical environment	0	15	11.01.99	29.01.99	NA
1.7.2 Analyze system load	0	15	11.01.99	29.01.99	NA
1.7.3 Determine software	0	15	11.01.99	29.01.99	NA
1.7.4 Determine hardware	0	20	01.02.99	26.02.99	NA
1.7.5 Network (LAN, WAN)	0	20	01.02.99	26.02.99	NA
1.8 Training	0	55	15.02.99	30.04.99	NA
1.8.1 Discuss training needs for SC and PT members	0	55	15.02.99	30.04.99	NA
1.8.2 Check on external and internal training possibilities	0	55	15.02.99	30.04.99	NA
1.8.3 Organize external or internal trainings	0	55	15.02.99	30.04.99	NA
1.8.4 Learn SAP functions	0	55	15.02.99	30.04.99	NA
1.9 Project control	0	20	05.04.99	30.04.99	NA
1.9.1 Organization of internal controlling	0	20	05.04.99	30.04.99	NA
1.9.2 Organization of external controlling	0	20	05.04.99	30.04.99	NA
1.9.3 Organization of progress control	0	20	05.04.99	30.04.99	NA
1.9.4 Organize time control	0	20	05.04.99	30.04.99	NA
1.10 Risk management	0	20	05.04.99	30.04.99	NA
1.10.1 Risk identification	0	20	05.04.99	30.04.99	NA
1.10.2 Risk analysis	0	20	05.04.99	30.04.99	NA
1.10.3 Risk response	0	20	05.04.99	30.04.99	NA
1.11 Change management	0	20	05.04.99	30.04.99	NA
1.11.1 Discuss change management actions	0	20	05.04.99	30.04.99	NA
1.11.2 Develop change management strategy	0	20	05.04.99	30.04.99	NA

Figure A.9 Detailed implementation schedule (*cont.*).

Task name	Compl (%)	Duration (days)	Start	Finish	Actual finish
1.12 Interfaces and conversions	0	55	15.02.99	30.04.99	NA
1.12.1 Define interfaces to other systems	0	55	15.02.99	30.04.99	NA
1.12.2 Design interfaces to other modules	0	55	15.02.99	30.04.99	NA
1.12.3 Design conversion of open orders	0	55	15.02.99	30.04.99	NA
1.12.4 Set up rough conversion plan	0	55	15.02.99	30.04.99	NA
1.13 Audit planning phase	0	0	30.04.99	30.04.99	NA
2 Realization phase	0	86	04.05.99	31.08.99	NA
2.1 Organizational structure	0	1	04.05.99	04.05.99	NA
2.1.1 Set up organizational structure acc. 1.6.2	0	1	04.05.99	04.05.99	NA
2.2 Customizing basics	0	3	04.05.99	06.05.99	NA
2.2.1 User maintenance	0	3	04.05.99	06.05.99	NA
2.2.2 Customize organizational structure	0	3	04.05.99	06.05.99	NA
2.2.3 Customize material master data	0	3	04.05.99	06.05.99	NA
2.2.4 Customize customer master data	0	3	04.05.99	06.05.99	NA
2.2.5 Classification	0	3	04.05.99	06.05.99	NA
2.2.6 Factory calendar	0	3	04.05.99	06.05.99	NA
2.3 Customizing specials	0	80	10.05.99	27.08.99	NA
2.3.1 Module specific customizing	0	80	10.05.99	27.08.99	NA
2.4 Conversion and interfaces	0	30	05.07.99	13.08.99	NA
2.4.1 Define interfaces to other systems	0	30	05.07.99	13.08.99	NA
2.4.2 Design interfaces to other modules	0	30	05.07.99	13.08.99	NA
2.4.3 Design conversion of open orders	0	30	05.07.99	13.08.99	NA
2.4.4 Set up conversion handbook	0	30	05.07.99	13.08.99	NA
2.4.5 Test conversion and interfaces	0	30	05.07.99	13.08.99	NA
2.6 Forms	0	30	05.07.99	13.08.99	NA
2.5.1 Gather requirements of forms needed	0	30	05.07.99	13.08.99	NA
2.5.2 Design forms	0	30	05.07.99	13.08.99	NA
2.5.3 Program forms	0	30	05.07.99	13.08.99	NA

Figure A.9 Detailed implementation schedule (*cont.*).

Task name		Compl (%)	Duration (days)	Start	Finish	Actual finish
	2.5.4 Test forms	0	30	05.07.99	13.08.99	NA
	2.5.5 Get user acceptance	0	30	05.07.99	13.08.99	NA
2.6	*Reports*					
	2.6.1 Gather requirements of reports needed	0	30	05.07.99	13.08.99	NA
	2.6.2 Design reports	0	30	05.07.99	13.08.99	NA
	2.6.3 Program reports	0	30	05.07.99	13.08.99	NA
	2.6.4 Test reports	0	30	05.07.99	13.08.99	NA
	2.6.5 Get user acceptance	0	30	05.07.99	13.08.99	NA
2.7	*Authorizations*					
	2.7.1 Gather requirement from line manager	0	10	09.08.99	20.08.99	NA
	2.7.2 Set up authorizations	0	10	09.08.99	20.08.99	NA
	2.7.3 Test authorizations	0	10	09.08.99	20.08.99	NA
	2.7.4 Transport authorizations to productive system	0	10	09.08.99	20.08.99	NA
2.8	*Prototype*					
	2.8.1 Set up test procedure	0	12	16.08.99	31.08.99	NA
	2.8.2 Test prototype	0	12	16.08.99	31.08.99	NA
	2.8.3 Get user acceptance	0	12	16.08.99	31.08.99	NA
3	**Preparation phase**	0	43	01.09.99	29.10.99	NA
3.1	*Planning productive system*					
	3.1.1 Verify implementation schedule	0	22	01.09.99	30.09.99	NA
	3.1.2 Check user and project member availability	0	22	01.09.99	30.09.99	NA
	3.1.3 Recalculate expected system load	0	22	01.09.99	30.09.99	NA
	3.1.4 Build up hardware if necessary	0	23	01.09.99	30.09.99	NA
3.2	*User documentation*					
	3.2.1 Create/update manuals	0	22	01.09.99	30.09.99	NA
	3.2.2 Update other module documentation	0	22	01.09.99	30.09.99	NA
3.3	*Productive environment set-up*					
	3.3.1 Check hardware and software	0	22	01.09.99	30.09.99	NA
	3.3.2 Customize productive system	0	22	01.09.99	30.09.99	NA

Figure A.9 Detailed implementation schedule (*cont.*).

Task name	Compl (%)	Duration (days)	Start	Finish	Actual finish
3.4 Reorganization and archiving					
3.4.1 Set up reorganization and archiving procedures	0	22	01.09.99	30.09.99	NA
3.4.2 Customize reorganization and archiving	0	22	01.09.99	30.09.99	NA
3.4.3 Test reorganization and archiving procedures	0	22	01.09.99	30.09.99	NA
3.5 System administration					
3.5.1 Set up application management	0	22	01.09.99	30.09.99	NA
3.5.2 Write application manual	0	22	01.09.99	30.09.99	NA
3.6 User training	0	43	01.09.99	29.10.99	NA
3.6.1 Check user availability for training	0	22	01.09.99	30.09.99	NA
3.6.2 Set up training schedule	0	22	01.09.99	30.09.99	NA
3.6.3 Prepare training documentation	0	22	01.09.99	30.09.99	NA
3.6.4 Prepare training environment	0	22	01.09.99	30.09.99	NA
3.6.5 Carry out training sessions	0	21	01.10.99	29.10.99	NA
3.7 Integration tests	0	43	01.09.99	29.10.99	NA
3.7.1 Set up test schedule	0	22	01.09.99	30.09.99	NA
3.7.2 Define test data	0	22	01.09.99	30.09.99	NA
3.7.3 Prepare system environment	0	22	01.09.99	30.09.99	NA
3.7.4 Carry out integration test	0	21	01.10.99	29.10.9	NA
3.8 Data transfer to productive system	0	43	01.09.99	29.10.99	NA
3.8.1 Check project member availability for weekend work	0	22	01.09.99	30.09.99	NA
3.8.2 Set up conversion time schedule	0	22	01.09.99	30.09.99	NA
3.8.3 Carry out conversion acc. to 2.4	0	21	01.10.99	29.10.99	NA
3.8.4 Transport reports and documents	0	21	01.10.99	29.10.99	NA
3.9 Manual data maintenance and entry	0	21	01.10.99	29.10.99	NA
3.9.1 Check stock entry	0	21	01.10.99	29.10.99	NA
3.10 Quality check productive system	0	21	01.10.99	29.10.99	NA
3.10.1 Set up and check test plan	0	21	01.10.99	29.10.99	NA
3.11 Release system for operational start	0	0	29.10.99	29.10.99	NA

Figure A.9 Detailed implementation schedule (*cont.*).

Task name	Compl (%)	Duration (days)	Start	Finish	Actual finish
4 Productive phase	0	175	01.11.99	30.06.00	NA
4.1 System optimization	0	45	01.11.99	31.12.99	NA
4.1.1 Optimize system settings	0	45	01.11.99	31.12.99	NA
4.1.2 Optimize technical operations	0	45	01.11.99	31.12.99	NA
4.2 Post-project activities	0	129	04.01.00	30.06.00	NA
4.2.1 Initiate follow-up projects	0	129	04.01.00	30.06.00	NA
4.2.2 Finalize project goals	0	129	04.01.00	30.06.00	NA
4.2.3 Improve processes and procedures	0	129	04.01.00	30.06.00	NA

Figure A.9 Detailed implementation schedule (*cont.*).

AUTHORIZATION REQUEST FORM

User: KO Department: Sales administration Location: Dreieich	PT responsible: BE Line manager: HK

Default settings   **Startmenu (Tcode/title):** ZS01 (own created area menu)
Printer: DE01

User parameters: Order type = AAT = OR   Inquiry type = AFT = IN
                          Quotation type = AGT = QT   Company code = BUK = 0001
                          Sched. agreement type = LPA = SA   Model division = RSP = 99
                          Ref. sales organization = RVK = 0001   Ref. distribution channel = RVT = 01
                          Sales office = VKB = 0001   Sales organization = VKO = 0001
                          Distribution channel = VTW = 01   Credit control area = KKB = 0001
                          Operating concern = ERB = 0001

User menu: Name: No longer required when 'Area Menu' is available

Organizational authorizations for	Company code:	0001
	Sales organization:	0001
	Plant:	na
	Sales office:	0001
	Sales group:	Related to SO 0001
	Purchasing organization:	na
	Account group:	na
	Controlling area:	0001
	Others:	

Date:	To be ready by:
Approval line manager:	Approval PT member:
Created by:	Ready date:

Figure A.10   Authorization request form.

Tcode	Transaction description
VA01	Create sales order
VA02	Change sales order/print order confirmation/display order changes
VA03	Display sales order
VA05	List sales order
VA11	Create inquiry
VA12	Change inquiry
VA13	Display inquiry
VA15	List inquiry
VA22	Change quotation/print quotation confirmation
VA23	Display quotation
VA25	List quotations
VA31	Create scheduling agreement
VA32	Change scheduling agreement/print agreement confirmation
VA33	Display scheduling agreement
VA35	List scheduling agreements
VD01	Create customer
VD02	Change customer
VD03	Display customer
VD04	Display customer account changes
VD05	Block/unblock customer
XD03	Display customer(incl FI data)
XD04	Display customer account changes(incl FI data)
FD33	Display customer credit management
FBL5	Display customer line items
MM03	Display material
V-51	Create price condition (PR00), include create w/reference, change, display, print condition overview
VD51	Create customer material info record
VD52	Change customer material info record
VD53	Display customer material info record
VD54	Selection of customer material info records by material
VL03	Display and print delivery note
VL04	Display delivery due list
VL05	List deliveries
VF01	Create invoice (pro forma only, F5 and F8)
VF02	Change invoice (pro forma only, F5 and F8)
VF03	Display and print invoice (customer related, F2/F5/F8/G2/L2/RE)
VF05	List invoices (customer related)
V.10	Ranking of top materials
V.11	Ranking of top customers
SO02	Outbox
SO03	Private folders
SO04	Shared folders
VC/1	List partner information
VC/2	List sales summary
KE12	Display plan data
KE30	Run profitability report

Figure A.10 Authorization request form (*cont.*).

Function area	Function description	Transaction	Notes about change	Subsequent action	Responsibility	Date
Customizing	Create sales order/text	VA01	Customer material info text is copied from the info record into order item	Check with plant possibility to use this text for CSS Check further usage of CSS text Determine implementation date Install correct text procedure and access sequence Document for users to get CSS numbers reset	HA	
Customizing	Implementation projects	SPRO	Sekal has created two projects. Unclear how to use these projects	IMG project 101 created. Data entries still to maintain. Still to get updated on handling of IMG projects (see SAP Docu)	HA, BE	
Customizing	Text determination	VOTX	Information upon after changing the texts when saving following message 'Please use the manual shipment connection Message no. VC 247'	Check what this means	BE	
Customizing	Text determination	VOTX	Text ideas are overwritten	Update text determination: – customer: SD: text type, text procedures – sales document: header and item: text types	HA	
Document flow	Copying from document to document	VTAA	Eventually copying control is different between production and test system	Compare copying control between production and test system + update if needed	HA, XDH	
Document flow	Create delivery/text	VL01	Text lines are blocked	Check settings in copying	HA, BE	

Figure A.11   Test procedure for migration.

Function area	Function description	Transaction	Notes about change	Subsequent action	Responsibility	Date
Document flow	Create KA and KR with reference to a claim document (ZCxx)	VA01	Copying from claim into KA/KR not supported	Install copying control for this flow	HA	
Document flow	Create KA document with reference to KB document	VA01	Copying control in Table TVCPAAK for copying KA KB E1 not supported. Message no. V1473. Despite this the KA document can be created correctly. No incompletion log. Incorrect schedule line category determined (F1 should be F0)	Update copying control. Replace schedule line category F1 by F0 within customizing category	HA	
Document flow	Create returns delivery for KA document	VL01	No quantities are copied into delivery and cannot be entered into delivery	Verify and correct settings into delivery	BE	
F8	Create pro forma for deliveries	VF01	No comments			
FD	Sample order	VA01	Two FD document types in system: 1. Delivery free of charge, 2. Free of charge delivery (presently in use)	Only one document type FD may exist. Verify why there are two equal document types available now and correct settings	HA, BE	

Figure A.11 Test procedure for migration (*cont.*).

ID	Task name	Compl (%)	Duration (days)	Start	Finish	Actual finish	Responsibility names	Comment
1	1 **Planning phase**	80	44	03.02.99	03.04.99	NA		
2	1.1 Decide which data must be available and how	100	10	03.02.99	12.02.99	12.02.99	HA, BE, XDH[0]	Sales through COPA/Orders through SIS/all XXL downloads
3	1.2 Have these downloads or prints available	100	3	10.02.99	12.02.99	12.02.99	HA, BE, XDH[0]	3 books with ABAP reports/SIS5010, variant Z95RS
4	1.3 Info to EL about document numbers to archive	100	1	24.02.99	24.02.99	24.02.99	BE	
5	1.4 Verify if any changes in PROD are required	100	17	03.02.99	25.02.99	25.02.99	BE, HA	Only ZSORC008
6	1.5 Get updated on consequences of archiving	100	3	03.03.99	05.03.99	05.03.99	BE, HA	
7	1.6 Reorganization of material master	100	5	03.03.99	07.03.99	07.03.99	BE, HA	MM70/MM71
8	1.7 Plan release test	100	1	10.03.99	10.03.99	10.03.99	BE, HA	1-4.4 test planned
9	1.8 Verify correct functionality	100	5	10.03.99	14.03.99	14.03.99	BE, HA	COPA and SIS problems (table inconsistencies) (file test03)
10	1.9 Get updated on IMG usage/projects within SAP	100	11	13.03.99	02.04.99	02.04.99	BE, HA	Not 100% clear yet, SAP docu to study ongoing
11	1.10 Create SD release change project within SAP	100	2	01.04.99	02.04.99	02.04.99	BE, HA	Project 101 created
12	1.11 Study release notes	0	12	19.03.99	03.04.99	NA	BE, HA	Printed, partially studied, ongoing

Figure A.12 Time schedule for migration.

ID	Task name	Compl (%)	Duration (days)	Start	Finish	Actual finish	Responsibility names	Comment
13	**2 Initial release test**	78	4	01.04.99	04.04.99	NA		
14	2.1 Correct text determination	100	4	01.04.99	04.04.99	04.04.99	BE, HA	
15	2.2 Area menus and authorizations	100	4	01.04.99	04.04.99	04.04.99	BE, HA	Work on user-ID sales users
16	2.3 SAP office	100	4	01.04.99	04.04.99	04.04.99	BE, HA	
17	2.4 Customer master	100	4	01.04.99	04.04.99	04.04.99	BE, HA	
18	2.5 Material master	100	4	01.04.99	04.04.99	04.04.99	BE, HA	
19	2.6 Price master	100	4	01.04.99	04.04.99	04.04.99	BE, HA	
20	2.7 Info record	100	4	01.04.99	04.04.99	04.04.99	BE, HA	
21	2.8 Payment and delivery terms	100	4	01.04.99	04.04.99	04.04.99	BE, HA	TVZBT and TINCT
22	2.9 OR flow	100	4	01.04.99	04.04.99	04.04.99	BE, HA	
23	2.10 ZSTO/ZSOR flow	100	4	01.04.99	04.04.99	04.04.99	BE, HA	
24	2.11 KB/KE flow	100	4	01.04.99	04.04.99	04.04.99	BE, HA	
25	2.12 Scheduling agreements	100	4	01.04.99	04.04.99	04.04.99	BE, HA	
26	2.13 DL flow	100	4	01.04.99	04.04.99	04.04.99	BE, HA	
27	2.14 Inventory management	100	4	01.04.99	04.04.99	04.04.99	BE, HA	
28	2.15 Invoicing/pro-forma	100	4	01.04.99	04.04.99	04.04.99	BE, HA	
29	2.16 Stock overview	100	4	01.04.99	04.04.99	04.04.99	BE, HA	
30	2.17 Classification	100	4	01.04.99	04.04.99	04.04.99	BE, HA	
31	2.18 SIS reports	100	4	01.04.99	04.04.99	04.04.99	BE, HA	
32	2.19 ABAP reports	100	4	01.04.99	04.04.99	04.04.99	BE, HA	
33	2.20 COPA reports	100	4	01.04.99	04.04.99	04.04.99	BE, HA	
34	2.21 Standard SAP reports/lists	100	4	01.04.99	04.04.99	04.04.99	BE, HA	
35	2.22 Activities acc to IMG release change project	100	4	04.04.99	04.04.99	04.04.99	BE, HA	

Figure A.12 Time schedule for migration (*cont.*).

ID	Task name	Compl (%)	Duration (days)	Start	Finish	Actual finish	Responsibility names	Comment
36	2.23 FD flow	0	4	01.04.99	04.04.99	NA	BE, HA	Not possible as doctype FD exists twice
37	2.24 Claims, credit-debit-returns memo requests	0	4	01.04.99	04.04.99	NA	BE, HA	Not possible as doctypes CR and DR exist twice
38	2.25 Background jobs	0	4	01.04.99	04.04.99	NA	BE, HA	
39	2.26 Print functions	0	4	01.04.99	04.04.99	NA	BE, HA	
40	2.27 Forms in general (OC, delivery note, invoice, IWF, claim)	0	4	01.04.99	04.04 97	NA	BE, HA	
41	2.28 List changes, additions, problems, shortcomings	0	4	01.04.99	04.04.99	NA	XDH, BE, HA	File TEST30F.doc
42	3 **Decide how to proceed**	86	2	08.04.99	09.04.99	NA		
43	3.1 Have outstanding activities listed	100	2	08.04.99	08.04.99	08.04.99	HA, BE, XDH	
44	3.2 List priority per activity	100	2	08.04.99	08.04.99	08.04.99	HA, BE	
45	3.3 List time availability support responsibilities	100	2	08.04.99	08.04.99	08.04.99	HA, BE, XDH	
46	3.4 Verify productive startdate	100	0	08.04.99	08.04.99	08.04.99	HA, BE	
47	3.5 Info to NW about productive startdate	0	1	09.04.99	09.04.99	NA	HA	Send mail to NW; CC to: MEP, EL, DH, HD, KvB, KGW
48	4 **Actions to carry out to get productive**	0	92	08.04.99	14.08.99	NA		
49	4.1 Finance	100	0	08.04.99	08.04.99	08.04.99		
50	4.1.1 Info to Mep about currency problems	100	0	08.04.99	08.04.99	08.04.99	BE	

Figure A.12 Time schedule for migration (*cont.*).

Index

administration of project 46–58
  information and
      communication 54–5
    bulletins 54–5
    marketing project 54
  meeting management 50–4
    agenda 50–1
    etiquette 52–3
    minutes of 53–4
    preparation for, useful tips 52
    project team meetings 54
  progress reporting 49
  project facilities 55–6
  project handbook 56
  project standards 56
  reporting 46–9
    frequency 49
  time recording 49–50
    sheet for 48
  weekly reporting 46–9
    procedure 47–9
    purpose 46–7
advanced business application
    programming (ABAP) 3
  program request 72–3
allocation policy, investigating
    96–7
ALVEO company profile 1–2
archiving
  in preparation phase 84–5
  tool for 84–5
as-is concept in planning phase
    62–3
  description 63
assimilation points and coping with
    change 122–3
authorization
  in as-is concept 63

in realization phase 80–1
request form 171–2
in to-be concept 66

big bang implementation 8–9
  threats arising 9
business-process re-engineering
    (BPR) 91–9
  after implementation 91–2,
    139
  allocation policy, investigating
    96
  core material numbers, reducing
    97–8
  customer matrix, defining 94–5
  elements of 92–3
  foaming and cross-linking,
    planning for 98
  functions and tasks, clarifying
    96
  lead-time reduction, plan for 96
  performance measurements,
    defining 95
  projects 93–9
  self-collectors, reducing 96
  small orders, processing 99
  start up losses, reducing 97–8
  stock held, decreasing 97
  supply chain management,
    improving 99

chairman of steering committee
    30
change management 7, 119–125
  coping with change 122–4
  negative, change as 120–1
  positive, change as 121–2
  preparation for change 119–120

closing phase of project 126–31
  analysis 126
  documentation 126
  handing over 126–30
    reintegration of project
        members 130–1
    SAP coordination organization
        127–9
    tasks and responsibilities
        129–30
communication
  and change management 120,
      123
  in initiation phase 15
  and internationalization of
      project 12
  in multi-site environment 11
  in planning phase 54–5
    bulletins 54–5
    marketing project 54
  by project manager 32, 33
company growth and initiation
    phase 15
competition in initiation phase 15
complexity of project 13–14
concepts in planning phase 61–9
  as-is 62–3
  to-be 63–8
consultants/consulting
  for conversion process 77
  improvement in 139
  in multi-site environment 11
  in planning phase 36–40
    choice of 37–8
    evaluation of 36–7
    as human resource component
        25, 26, 27
    internal 39–40
    pricing and budgeting 38–9,
        41
    tasks and responsibilities 37
  in risk analysis 114
control of project 7, 106–12
  cycle of 106–8
    coaching 108
    correcting 107–8
    defining 106
    measuring 107
  external 108–9

  internal 108
  issue list 109
  monitoring 109–10
  organization of 108–9
  regular, continuous 139–40
  time control 111
conversions
  in realization phase 76–8
    considerations for 76–7
    handbook 78
    project 77–8
    ready on time 139
  in to-be concept 66
core material numbers, reducing
    97–8
costs
  analysis of 144–7
  of resources in planning phase
      40–4
    of consultants 38–9
    estimating 44
    external, budgeting 40–3
    internal 43
  transparency in initiation phase
      15
cultural differences and
    internationalization of project
    12–13
customer matrix, defining 94–5
customer service 15
customising in realization phase
    76
  forms 79

data accuracy in implementation
    133
data transfer in preparation phase
    86
deadlines
  implementation after 148
  implementation before 150
  importance of 20
  principles 148

efficient organization of project
    22–4
enterprise resource planning 3–4
external costs, budgeting in
    planning phase 40–3

external project control 108–9
external training 104–5

facilities for administration in
    planning phase 55–6
financial incentives for human
    resources in planning phase
    28–9
foaming and cross-linking,
    planning for 98
follow-up projects after productive
    phase 99–101
forms in realization phase 78–9
    programming 79
framework of project 5–14
    implementation strategy 7–11
    inter-company projects 12
    internationalization 12–13
    as multi-site environment 11
    project complexity 13–14
    project life cycle 5–7
    special characteristics 11–14
FuturA 15, 18
    bulletin 164–5

going live preparation 86–8
    project members on 87
    start date 86–7
    technical preparation 87–8
        hardware 87
        software 88

handbook 56
    conversions and interfaces 77,
        78
hardware
    in planning phase 70–1, 74
        SAP server 70–1
        WAN 71
    preparation 87
    in risk analysis 115
hierarchies in project organization
    23
human resources 25–36
    enlisting consultants *see*
        consultants/consulting
    hiring new people 25
    incentives for 28–9

information technology team
    35–6
    in multi-site environment 11
    participation of 26–7
    project manager 30–3
    project secretary 33
    project team 34–5
    provision of 25
    quality of 26
    steering committee 29–30
        chairman 30
        tasks and responsibilities 29
        top management participation
            29–30
    temporary staff 25
    and trust 27–8

identification of risk 112–14
implementation plan 58–61
    factors for 137–40
    management software for 59
    schedule for 58–9, 60, 166–70
    special problems 132–6
        data accuracy 133
        material master maintenance
            132
        production methods 134–5
        program errors 133
        SAP-X extension 135–6
implementation strategy 7–11
    overview 10
incentives for human resources in
    planning phase 28–9
inefficient organization of project
    21–2
information
    and change management 120,
        123
    in initiation phase 15
    open policy 138
    in planning phase 54–5
        bulletins 54–5
        marketing project 54
    for project administration 47
information technology
    in BPR 91–2
    team
        in planning phase 35–6
        in project organization 24

initiation phase 15–16
integration test in preparation
    phase 86
interfaces
    in as-is concept 63
    in realization phase 76–8
        considerations for 76–7
        handbook 78
        project 77–8
        ready on time 139
    in to-be concept 66
internal consulting 39–40
internal project control 108
internal training 104–5
internationalization of project
    12–13
    in multi-site environment 11
investment costs, budgeting in
    planning phase 40–1
issue list in project control 109

lead-time reduction, plan for 96
line-specific training of project
    members 104

make-to-order production in
    implementation 134–5
make-to-stock production in
    implementation 134–5
management team
    and change management 119
    minutes, form 163
    in multi-site environment 11
    in planning phase 34
    in project organization 23
    and SAP coordination
        organization 127
    size of 22
    strong and effective 138
material master maintenance in
    implementation 132
meeting management
    in planning phase 50–4
        agenda 50–1, 160–1
        etiquette 52–3
        minutes of 53–4
        preparation for, useful tips 52
        project team meetings 54
        time limits 51

for project team 54
in SAP coordination
    organization 130
Microsoft Project 59
migration
    test procedure for 173–4
    time schedule for 175–7
modules
    coordinators in closing phase
        128–9
        tasks and responsibilities 129
    management of 66
monitoring project control 109–10
multi-site environment of project
    11

naming conventions in planning
    phase 73
non-financial benefits of project
    151–2

objectives of project 18–20
    analysis 140–4
    definitions 18–20
    simple, clear and measurable
        138
    success, measurements 18
on-line access in initiation phase
    15
on-line availability of data 85
optimizing system 90–1
organization of project 21–4
    clear and simple 138
    detailed plan 156
    efficient 22–4
    inefficient 21–2
    in meetings agenda 51

performance measurements 63
    defining 95
planning phase 6, 17–74
    concepts 61–9
        as-is 62–3
        to-be 63–8
    definition of project 17–18
    implementation plan 58–61
        management software for 59
        schedule for 58–9, 60
    objectives of project 18–20

definitions 18–20
success, measurements 18
organization of project 21–4
  efficient 22–4
  hierarchies 23
  inefficient 21–2
project administration *see*
    administration of project
resources 24–46
  consulting *see* consultants/
    consulting
  costs *see* costs
  human resources *see* human
    resources
scope of project 17–21
strategy of project 20
technical environment 69–74
  hardware 70–1, 74
  software 72–4
preparation phase 6, 83–9
  archiving 84–5
  data, on-line availability 85
  data transfer 86
  going live 86–8
    hardware preparation 87
    project members on 87
    software preparation 88
    start date 86–7
    technical preparation 87–8
  integration test 86
  user manual 83–4
  user support 84
production methods in
    implementation 134–5
productive phase 7, 90–101
  business-process re-engineering
    91–9
    after implementation 91–2
    elements of 92–3
    projects of 93–9
  follow-up projects 99–101
  optimizing 90–1
program errors in implementation
    133
progress control 43
progress reporting 162
  in meetings agenda 51
project analysis 140–51
  costs/savings 144–7

non-financial benefits 151–2
  objectives 140–4
  strategy 144
  throughput time 147–51
project leader/manager
  in planning phase 30–3
    as human resource component
      26, 27
    skills needed 31
    tasks and responsibilities 30–1
    useful tips for 31–3
  in project control 108
  report form 157
project members
  full-time 138
  line-specific training 104
  in planning phase
    as human resource component
      26, 27
  project-management-specific
    training 104
  qualified 138
  reintegration of after closing
    phase 130–1
  report form 158
  support, in risk analysis 114
  system specific training 103–4
  trust among 137
project secretary 33
project standards in planning
    phase 56
project team
  meetings 54
  in planning phase 34–5
    composition of 25–6
  in project organization 24
project-management-specific
    training of project members
    104
prototyping in realization phase
    81

realization phase 6, 75–82
  authorization in 80–1
  conversions and interfaces 76–8
    considerations for 76–7
    handbook 78
    project 77–8
  customising 76

realization phase (*cont.*)
  forms 78–9
  model organizational structure
    75–6
  prototyping 81
  reports 79–80
report forms
  in as-is concept 63
  authorization request form
    171–2
  progress reporting 162
  project leader 157
  project management team
    minutes 163
  project members 158
  in to-be concept 66
  weekly, summary 159
reporting
  needs in realization phase 79–80
  in planning phase 46–9
    frequency 49
    procedure 47–9
    progress reporting 49
    purpose 46–7
    weekly 46–9
  on progress 162
  in SAP coordination
    organization 130
report-request form 80
reports in realization phase 79–80
resignation, risk of 113, 115,
  117–18
resources
  in planning phase 24–46
  consulting *see* consultants/
    consulting
  costs *see* costs
  human resources *see* human
    resources
response to risk 114–15
risk management 7, 112–19
  analysis of risk 113, 114
  experience of 115–17
  identification in project
    administration 47
  identification of risk 112–14
  resignation 113, 115, 117–18
  response to risk 114–15
roll-out implementation 9

running costs, budgeting in
  planning phase 42–3

SAP coordination team 127–8
  in closing phase 127–9
  administration of 130
  functions of 127–9
  tasks and responsibilities
    129–30
SAP R/3 package
  basic system 3–4
  implementation strategy 20
  server 70–1
SAP-X extension 135–6
  general description 135
savings analysis 144–7
scope of project 17–21
self-collectors, reducing 96
small orders, processing 99
software
  in planning phase 72–4
    ABAP program request 72–3
    naming conventions 73
    program changes 73
    programming guidelines 72
    for project management 59
    for to-be concept 64
  preparation 88
  in risk analysis 115
start up losses, reducing 97–8
steering committee
  in planning phase 29–30
  in project control 108
  in project organization 23
  training members 103
step-by-step implementation 7–8
  threats arising 8
stock held, decreasing 97
strategy of project 20
  analysis 144
supply chain management,
  improving 99
SWOT analysis 68
system specific training of project
  members 103–4

technical environment in planning
  phase 69–74
  hardware 70–1, 74

software 72–4
test procedure for migration
    173–4
throughput time
  analysis of 147–51
  short 23
time control 111
  in meetings agenda 51
time recording in planning phase
    49–50
  sheet for 48
time schedule for migration 175–7
time-zone differences and
    internationalization of project
    13
to-be concept in planning phase
    63–8
  consequences 68
  content, description of 65–8
    management summary 65
    performance measurements
      66–7
  as guideline for project 139
  purpose 63–4
  responsibility for 65
  software guidelines 64
top management
  involvment 22
  ownership of project 30, 137
  participation on steering
      committee 29–30

training 7, 102–6
  and change management 120,
      123
  costs of 43
  internal vs external 104–5
  project members 103–4
    line-specific 104
    project-management-specific
      104
    system specific 103–4
  steering committee members
      103
  users 102–3
travelling costs
  and internationalization of
      project 13
trust
  among project members
      137
  in planning phase 27–8
  in project manager 32

user acceptance, in risk analysis
    115
user manual in preparation phase
    83–4
user support in preparation phase
    84

Wide Area Network 71
  costs of 43